DATE DUE

OC 29 '96			
MR 20 '97			
MY 6 '97			
AY 5 '97			
DE 3 '97			
MY 7 '99			
AP 15 '00			
JE 5 '01			
OC 17 '01			
NO 14 '01			
DE 11 '01			

DEMCO 38-296

*Smart
Women
Smart
Moves*

Smart
Women
Smart
Moves

Vanessa J. Weaver, Ph.D.
and Jan C. Hill

amacom

American Management Association

New York • Atlanta • Boston • Chicago • Kansas City • San Francisco • Washington, D.C.
Brussels • Mexico City • Tokyo • Toronto

This book is available at a special
discount when ordered in bulk quantities.
For information, contact Special Sales Department,
AMACOM, a division of American Management Association,
135 West 50th Street, New York, NY 10020.

This publication is designed to provide accurate and authoritative
information in regard to the subject matter covered. It is sold with
the understanding that the publisher is not engaged in rendering
legal, accounting, or other professional service. If legal advice or
other expert assistance is required, the services of a competent
professional person should be sought.

Library of Congress Cataloging-in-Publication Data

Weaver, Vanessa J.
    Smart women, smart moves / Vanessa J. Weaver and Jan C.
      Hill.
         p.   cm.
    Includes bibliographical references and index.
    ISBN 0-8144-0205-4
    1. Vocational guidance for women.   2. Job satisfaction.
    3. Women-Employment.   I. Hill, Jan C.   II. Title.
    HF5382.6.W43   1994
    331.7'02'082—dc20   94-4852
                                             CIP

Printing number

10 9 8 7 6 5 4 3 2 1

This is dedicated to my mother, Hildy, for teaching me to be strong in the face of adversity.

—Jan

This is to the women in my life:
  Emma F. Weaver, my mom
  Nicole D. Weaver-Christman, my daughter
  Emmalesha Weaver-Christman, my granddaughter
  Caryliss and Connie Weaver, my sisters
  And to the memory of my grandmother, Robie Lee Thomas
  —Vanessa

Contents

List of Figures

Acknowledgments

Together we'd like to thank:

> *Andrea Pedolsky,* our initial editor at AMACOM, for her energy and passion to get this book published—and for giving us a kick when we needed it!

> *Katherine Stackpoole,* for her patient editing and direct feedback.

> *Lovette Tucker,* for late nights and endless days of typing and retyping the manuscript, and for her candid feedback as well.

> *Floyd and Jackie Dickens,* for their belief in our vision and introduction to AMACOM.

> *All the women* who shared their stories and their insights with us—this book is richer for your efforts.

Jan would like to thank:

> *John Dye,* for the incentive to write this book—good things can come out of trying circumstances.

> *Lis and Maddy,* for all the support.

> *Tina,* for her Katie McGuire's coffee.

Vanessa would like to thank:

> *My parents, Emma and Manuel Weaver,* for their ongoing encouragement and support.

> *Jan Hill,* for being a great friend and colleague.

> *Dr. Robert L. Williams,* for the deeper understanding of why relationships are important and the realization that good things can come out of trying circumstances.

> *Dr. Dorothy I. Height and Dr. Alexis Herman,* for being wonderful role models and caring friends.

Introduction: A Tale of Two Women

They say that help comes from strange places, and certainly a White woman from Texas never expected to team up with a Black woman from St. Louis. But team up we did. We became friends in 1987 while we were both happily working at a Fortune 20 corporation. Over the ensuing years, our friendship deepened—and our satisfaction with our work lives diminished. We began to question how happy we truly were with our work and our relationships with our employer. We realized that if we were going to spend over fifty hours a week working, we wanted more out of it than we were getting. We had hit a crossroads in our relationships with work. We knew that something was going to have to change, but we weren't sure what.

As we talked about our increasing work frustrations and our hopes and dreams for work that is rewarding and fulfilling, we began to formulate a premise. It goes like this: Women approach work differently from men. We rarely view it as "just a job"; instead, we see it as a *relationship*. We want much more out of it than just a paycheck. We are searching for personal growth, feelings of accomplishment and self-actualization, recognition of our worth and contribution, support, challenge, even friendship and in some cases, love. Women take their careers to heart. Often we have sacrificed a great deal to have a career. Why settle for one that isn't meaningful? As a result, we enter into relationships with employers to sustain and nourish our careers. These relationships can be with an entire company or division, or with a manager who has power over the relationship.

Interestingly, we develop our work relationships in much the same way as we develop our intimate personal relationships. If you look closely, you can see all the signs and behaviors that are typically associated with stages like dating, going steady, getting engaged, getting married, or in some cases, becoming a mistress. They just play out a little differently at work. Haven't you heard expressions like: "She's married to that company—I don't think she'll ever leave"? Or have you noticed when people refer to themselves and their company as one entity, as in: "We are launching product x" or "We are hiring people right now"? It's no wonder, then, that the deeper a woman's commitment is to her work relationship, the more painful it can be when it goes awry.

Making the decision to stay in a troubled work relationship and improve it or leave it behind to form a more fulfilling work partnership elsewhere is no easy task. In fact, we know women who have battled unhappily with that dilemma for years. But the good news is that you have choices. By making choices, you responsibly manage your own life and dictate your own personal happiness. It is in your control.

Why This Book?

This book provides a chronicle of what we have discovered in our struggles to decide whether to stay with existing work relationships and improve them, or jettison them for more fulfilling relationships elsewhere. It is intended to help answer the questions that 56 million working women are asking:

- How can I find satisfaction at work?
- Is my company a good fit?
- Do we have a commitment to each other?
- Should I stay or should I go?
- How will I know if my choice is the right one?
- I know what I want to do. Can you tell me how to do it so I won't regret it?

Recent studies show that the vast majority of female workers dream about leaving or intend to leave their current jobs.[1] If you've been pulling your hair out over your work relationship, this book will help you make the choices that are necessary for you to find the satisfaction you've been longing for.

We made a decision early on to confine this work to what we know best—women's experiences in the workplace. Thus, we've written this book from a feminine perspective, and it is intended to help *women* wrestle with the challenges of pursuing a fulfilling work relationship. Our goal has been to create the sort of guidebook that we wish we had had when we went through our own work relationship challenges.

Nonetheless, we have often been questioned about how women's experiences differ from those of men, or whether it has been our intent to exclude men from our discussions in the book. We have shared our models, concepts, and tools with men we have worked with over the years. They unanimously agreed that the models make sense, and they were eager to converse in the feminine relationship language (spouse, mistress, etc.) as it related to their own careers. We encourage men to read this book so that they can better understand work relationship dynamics from a feminine point of view. The more sensitized we all become, the better equipped we are to create an environment that celebrates and leverages the combined talents of both women and men.

What Reading This Book Will Be Like

We hope that reading this book will be like spending time with a trusted friend. Psychologist Merle Shain wrote, "The job of a friend is not to decide what should be done. . . . The job of a friend is to understand, and to supply energy and hope, and in doing so to keep those they value on their feet a little longer, so that they can fight another round and grow stronger in themselves."[2] We don't intend to tell you what to do. Instead, we hope to help you find the path for yourself by sharing what we and others have learned along the bumpy road to career gratification.

This will be a personal discovery journey where you'll find out things about yourself that will help you forge better relationships in the workplace—and in your life in general. This book is about you, so we've built in plenty of room for you to express and understand your own thoughts and feelings. We've included several short quizzes and written exercises to help guide you through the book. And because we've found that women learn by sharing stories, you'll find lots of real life stories throughout.

We've taken an eclectic approach to this book; you'll find words of wisdom from famous women as well as from smart women unknown by the world at large. We'll cite examples and ideas from experts and psychologists, as well as personal examples from women who are our friends. We don't espouse one right way to make the decision that's right for you. Instead, we offer suggestions, quizzes, exercises, and techniques that may work for you. Choose what works, and use it to your advantage. To get the most out of this book, take time for yourself, relax, and be truthful.

Our Commitment

We have a sincere commitment to helping other women make their unique contributions to the world. We believe that every woman should be able to revel in the satisfaction that accompanies accomplishment, contribution, and personal growth in every aspect of life. We hope that this book will give you the answers you need to negotiate for the work relationship you want and deserve. It is our sincere wish that by sharing what we've learned—on our own and from the grace of other Smart Women—we can help you on your journey to becoming the person you most want to be.

Regardless of whether you ultimately choose to stay in your work relationship or leave it, the relationship will be altered in some way. Although we both left our employers, we are now married to our own entrepreneurial enterprises. The lessons we have learned came from our decisions to leave an established work relationship and commit to a new work relationship elsewhere. So that you may know us better, here briefly are our stories.

Jan's Story

Having lived in corporate America for over a decade, I've developed a certain reverence for statistics. I've been carefully trained in the art of finding facts to back up my instincts. So imagine my excitement when I came across an article that announced that "eight out of ten career women dream about changing occupations—nearly half have done so, and for most the change has been for the better."[3] Unfortunately, I didn't discover that truthful revelation until after I had left my organization. In fact, not many of the articles or facts that women in corporations religiously copied and faxed to each other told me anything of what I wanted to hear when I was going through my own decision to break free of my work relationship. Nothing told me that I wasn't losing my mind, that what I was feeling was a natural part of my personal growth (not decline!), or that I was not alone.

Instead, I found myself donning the uniform of suit, pantyhose, and pumps, applying extra makeup to cover the bags under my eyes from overwork and underenjoyment, and boldly going forth each day hoping for a change of attitude.

By most measures I was extremely successful. I was working for a Fortune 20 company, had moved through five assignments in the past ten years, and had finally been told by the executive vice-president that I had what it took to succeed and become a general manager (a lofty level thus far achieved only by males). I was making top dollar, had a great house by the ocean, vacationed in exotic places. What more could a girl want? So why was it that the only tune I was humming was Peggy Lee's "Is That All There Is?"

Always garnering high points for my ability to manage others, I had even "saved" a female manager or two from leaving the organization. Then suddenly, at thirty-one, I faced my toughest managerial challenge: Saving myself. I'd been offered the brass ring, but something inside was telling me not to take it. The only thing I knew for sure was that I didn't want to be a fool—or be made a fool of.

After a painful but liberating journey of self-exploration, I finally opted to say good-bye to the corporation. Nothing prepared me for the devastation that followed. I discovered how much I had relied on my work relationship to give me value and meaning. I found out that some people whom I thought were my friends in the organization really weren't my friends once I was on the other side. I didn't understand why my managers and peers were angry and resentful at my leaving. I ended up with no business card, no paycheck, no insurance, no corporate identity.

Then I discovered what I really did have: I had myself back! I also had friends in unexpected places. I revived relationships with some of the women whom I had known earlier in my career. I sought out women who had pioneered a corporate career track and then had opted to leave. They had amazing insights to share, and our discussions proved to be therapeutic for us all. I began to write down what we had learned so that I could purge myself of negative thoughts and open up my mind to enjoy the glorious freedom I had earned for myself.

It's amazing how I can remember the day I left perfectly: May 9, 1990. I walked out of my office and boarded a plane for the Virgin Islands. For the first time in far too long, I was on my way to doing what I wanted to do! I remember feeling as if I had just walked out of a dark movie house into the brightness of day. I was bombarded by the sheer expanse of a glittering world with options I hadn't allowed myself even to imagine. I had no business plan to follow, no flowchart of expected events, no data bank to analyze. There was only me—and I liked it that way.

I had run a $350 million business unit and had supervised the careers of forty people, but found it difficult to spend time on myself and my own relationships. For the first time, I really felt on my own. There was no school curriculum, no corporate career path, no one telling me what to do and how to do it. And because those elements weren't there, there also wasn't any *thing* around to validate my choices. My friends and family looked on in wonderment and shock, waiting to see if I knew what I was doing.

Always liking to live on the edge, I had pushed myself to the brink. Vacillating between terror and euphoria, I slowly began to make sense out of what I had done. I was angry at "the corporation." I didn't feel that it had treated me well. I was confused at the put-downs of me because I left and wasn't doing what my coworkers had wanted me to do. On the one hand, I was excited to be free of "them," but on the other hand, I was petrified and unsure about my next move. I knew that I had to get over these competing emotions, and I ultimately chose to create another work relationship with a new company that respected my skills.

Ironically, this company's biggest client was the corporation I had just left. I still hadn't resolved my feelings about that association, so I ultimately found myself repeating the same issues. I wished I had continued to do my homework to discover that "only 8 percent of [women] are doing now what they expected to be doing when they started out."[4]

I left that work relationship after eight months, but I had learned what I needed to learn. I began teaching myself how to make choices based on my values and principles—on what I wanted for myself. I worked on living responsibly. It finally hit me that it's not about who's right and who's wrong in the work relationship. It's not about being fair. Life isn't about those things. It's about choice and personal responsibility.

I recognized that I had a commitment to help women who were facing the same career quandries I was, and I began to make choices that supported that commitment. It was during this time that I began hearing from disgruntled female corporate climbers. They wanted to know what life was like on the other side. Was it what I expected? How did I know it was time to leave? I understood that they were looking for assurances that they weren't going crazy. I made a choice then to find a way to help them as others had helped me.

Those of us who have survived the ending of an important work relationship want to offer our assurances that there is a wonderful life on the other side. Making the choice to leave doesn't have to mean that you're selling out, maxed out, or burned out. It takes real courage to make a tough decision. It is a sign that you have taken responsibility for your own personal growth and that you know best what you are capable of and what you want to do.

During the breakup of my work relationship, I was blessed to have Vanessa as a mentor and a friend. We have marveled at the zigzag path we have taken to put ourselves in a position to help both women and their companies create more healthy working environments for everyone. Our consulting and seminar work, which is geared toward helping women achieve personal and professional success in the workplace, is the most rewarding work I have ever done. We are women learning to support other women, and it's about time.

My life is now rich with relationships and work I value, and I like myself again. I hope this book will provide you with the resources to find your true self again.

Vanessa's Story

Almost three years ago, I acted on my choice to have an amicable divorce from my corporate relationship of twelve and a half years. I've never regretted my decision; it was the right one for me. My life since that divorce is a testimony to good timing, planning, networking, and being prepared to take advantage of opportunities. I'd like to say it was a big testimony to risk taking, but I didn't perceive my risks to be that great at the time I left. I tried to eliminate uncertainty by planning for every contingency. There wasn't anything impulsive about this breakup. It was a win-win situation for me and my company. We didn't split with feelings of anger or resentment. Absent was the "they done me wrong" song. In fact, our relationship continues today in a different form: they're a valued client of my firm. My mentors and sponsors are still my biggest supporters.

Things haven't always run this smoothly. Years before I left, we went through some rocky times together. There was a period when I wanted to quit. I didn't care about being methodical or strategic. I just wanted out. I figured I would land on my feet and take my chances. Clearly, I was running away from a painful work relationship versus walking toward a better one.

During that time, I felt cheated. My stellar performances, my ability to accomplish multiple tasks exceptionally well, and my recognition as an up-and-coming star with a salary that doubled in almost three years were not enough for me to be admitted to the coveted inner circle. In the terms of our Feminine Relationship Model, introduced in Chapter 1, I felt as if I was a Fiancée, ready to tie the knot in marriage. But I learned that my organization had no intention of marrying me.

This revelation was followed by a tumultuous period of personal pain that lasted almost two years. I cried a lot. I stayed angry and wore a disconcerting frown to prove it. This was my shield. I felt helpless and out of control of everything in my career and my life, and I turned my anger inward. I gained weight because I would come home and eat everything in sight. I stayed sick. Seeing my doctor was a nightmare. He would always say, "Vanessa, this is nothing but stress. You should know this better than anyone." With a smile, he'd say, "Doctor, heal thyself!" I hated that!

I couldn't separate the pain I felt at work from the pain I felt at home. I brought my work woes home with me and repeated my story to anyone who would listen. In the beginning, my family and friends tried to be supportive. They listened and listened and listened. But I finally wore them out. At the same time, I was fading fast. I didn't have a lot of energy to give to anyone or anything else.

My best friend and supporter, my mom, changed my life at that critical point. The story is too long to share here, but the essence of it is that she told me to "get on with it!" The "with it" was getting very clear about my life's plan and how to support it with work relationships. She told me that this was to be the only topic of our conversation the next time we talked.

At first, I was angry because she was not willing to support my choice of misery (mind you, this was now a two-year choice). I felt she just didn't understand. The truth was that I didn't have a life's plan. Staying angry and blaming "them" was no longer justification for me not to have a plan. I felt naked and exposed. Mom and my friends provided incredible support. Eventually, I got "with it" and chose to get out of misery, stay with my work relationship, and make it work.

My decision to stay several more years was the right one. Had I not stayed, I wouldn't have learned the invaluable lessons of creating work relationships and experiences that support my life plan. This perspective changed the type of work relationships I wanted and needed. I went from being a Fiancée to choosing misery, to choosing a Mistress relationship—a comfortable choice for both me and my company.

For nine years this relationship was wonderful. I was in control of the most critical career decisions and made only those moves that supported my life's plan. I got promoted and received substantial pay increases. I established more supportive and trusting relationships with a diverse group of people. In short, I stayed and was happy.

Once I got past my period of misery, I paid more attention to my personal and social life. I successfully graduated my two daughters from high school and provided them with a college experience. Both of my daughters got married, I became a grandmother, I got married, and I relocated across the United States.

Once all the pieces began falling in place, it became clear that I had to venture out on my own, to make my life's plan come alive through my own company. I realized that my current work relationship had matured enough to allow both sides to get our needs met in different ways. We found a positive solution in letting go.

Now I celebrate my life. It's not that everything has been perfect. I've had to deal with other disappointments since I left. What has been key for me is that now I don't wallow long in misery when confronted with those disappointments, and that's a relief!

I also value the role of getting and giving support. It was the turning point for me. It's this support I want to give to you as you struggle with the decision to leave or stay with your work relationship. *Smart Women, Smart Moves* is intended to provide you with that support. Carry us with you at all times and lean on us when you need to. I hope you experience *Smart Women, Smart Moves* as Jan's and my gift of support to you.

Part I

Work Relationships— The Female Perspective

In our individual lives, relationships are one of the most important vehicles by which we create our identities and through which we define ourselves. . . . A relationship is a process and not a destination. It is not necessarily the final emotional resting place of the persons who enter it, but a vital and growing entity which has a life—and a lifetime—of its own.

Daphne Rose Kingma, *Coming Apart: Why Relationships End and How to Live Through the Ending of Yours*

The time has finally come when massive numbers of women are free to address their individual needs for accomplishment, contribution, growth, respect, and even self-actualization by creating a professional working identity. In the past, our dreams were centered around our contributions to our families, our mates, our homes. Generations of cultural training taught us that "a woman's place is in the home," and that we should be fulfilled by our relationships there. Certainly these relationships remain important, but many women have sensed a growing need to stretch beyond the homemaker role to explore other aspects of themselves. What began with career trailblazers from Susan B. Anthony and Mary McLeod Bethune to Betty Friedan, Hillary Rodham Clinton, and Maya Angelou has now become a boom of close to 60 million working women in the United States alone.

We are here to stay, and we have brought with us a host of dreams and expectations about the dimensions that work can bring into our lives. We are part of that exciting breakthrough time in history where one culture invades the land of another, and it is forever altered. Evidence of the feminization of the workplace is all around us, and so are signs of the woman's struggle. Every day we witness the impact of choices being made by our contemporaries. Whether it is Anita Hill requesting respect and propriety from a colleague, or Hillary Clinton bringing new meaning to the term "First Lady," or some advertiser's vision of the "perfect" working woman, we are constantly bombarded with an expanding array of choices.

Along with these exciting choices comes some confusion. Since we are a generation of pioneers in what has traditionally been male territory, there aren't volumes of women's wisdom to help us chart our own paths to fulfillment and sanity in our workplace roles. In fact, "The first generation of women to have lifelong full-time careers outside the home will [only] have 25 or 30 years of business experience around the year 2000."[1]

While we must admit this is progress, our collective business experience pales in comparison to our experience in developing meaningful personal relationships. We know how relationships work, and this knowledge can be a great asset to women in pursuit of a rewarding career. Whether we are developing a personal relationship with a mate or a work relationship with an organization or a particular manager, we follow a similar progressive pattern: we date, we go steady, we become engaged, and we get married. In some instances we aren't willing to make a long-term commitment to an organization, or the organization isn't willing to commit to us, and the result is that we become mistresses. If the relationship isn't working out at all, we may ultimately choose to leave the organization to pursue a more fulfilling relationship elsewhere. The key is that we know how these relationships work, and we form them as a way of getting our needs met in the workplace.

The challenge for women is that these work relationships don't occur in a vacuum; they are in addition to all of the other roles traditionally assigned to women. For example, remember that silly Enjoli perfume commercial with the woman dancing with a frying pan and singing, "I can bring home the bacon, fry it up in the pan, and never let you forget you're a man—because I'm a woman, W-O-M-A-N!". While many of us who have been around for a while can now laugh at that image, it does capture some of the expectations that society has of working women and some of the unrealistic expectations that we may have of ourselves. Moreover, these expectations have continually increased as we have realistically viewed the trade-offs, sacrifices, and detours we have had to make in the balancing act of juggling personal and work relationships. From delayed childbearing to loneliness or broken marriages, the price we have had to pay to stay in our work relationships has upped the ante of what we expect from these relationships. Most of the women we have worked with agree that they expect their work relationships to provide professional validation, contribute to self-esteem, and be a meaningful and fulfilling addition to their personal lives.

Having these wonderful work relationships is easier said than done. But one thing is certain: If we're going to continue to make sacrifices for our careers, or at the very least, be willing to invest eight hours a day Monday through Friday at work, then it behooves us to be in the driver's seat of our own careers. We do have choices. We can choose to invest energy to turn around a troubled work relationship or decide that it is best for us to divorce ourselves from the relationship completely. No one said that the choices would be easy, but we do have choices just the same.

The first step in making choices is to understand where you are now and why. Part One will give you a foundation for understanding the relationship you have with your organization, and it will help you determine whether your work relationship can meet your needs now and in the future.

In Chapter 1 you'll evaluate your work relationship based on the needs you are trying to fulfill, the investment and commitment you are willing to make, and the way you would describe the relationship you are currently in. Based on this assessment, you will know which of the five stages of work relationships you are currently in: Dating, Girlfriend, Mistress, Fiancée, or Spouse. You'll also gain insight into how relationships develop and change as your needs change. No doubt, these are issues that you have thought about in examining your personal relationships, but have you applied the same concepts to help you understand the dynamics of your work relationships?

Next, in Chapter 2, you'll examine your relationship from your organization's point of view. By evaluating the signals that management is sending you, you'll get a clearer definition of the relationship they want to have with you. By comparing the two viewpoints—yours and theirs—you'll see if any discontinuities exist that may be causing you discomfort and stress.

Consider this the first step in your journey of self-discovery. Now is the time to be selfish and take some time for yourself. Give yourself permission to take some afternoons, evenings, or weekends to get back in touch with your own needs. By the time you have completed the personal evaluations in Part One, you will have a greater understanding of any work issues that stand in the way of getting your needs met.

We promise that this will be a rewarding personal journey. We've been down this road, and although the discovery process for both of us was painful, the view from the other side is absolutely wonderful. Let us be the friends who can help you understand and can help you find energy and hope to make the choices necessary to fulfill your dreams.

1

It's More Than a Job; It's a Relationship

> It is our relationships, more than anything else in our lives, which help us accomplish the developmental tasks through which we define ourselves. That's why we choose the people [companies] we do and that's why they choose us. That's why relationships begin and end.
>
> Daphne Rose Kingma, *Coming Apart: Why Relationships End and How to Live Through the Ending of Yours*

As we struggle to create our professional identities, we naturally enter into relationships with our employers. These relationships may be with a company or an organization in the sense that it is an entity with its own culture, personality, and identity. Or we may center our attention on a particular manager who, we feel, holds the keys to our satisfaction with the organization. As women, our relationships with our employers tend to mirror the liaisons we pursue in our personal lives. These relationships pass through different stages as we strive to develop the one relationship that best meets our needs.

To see what we mean, take a few minutes to assess your own relationship with your employer by completing the Work Relationship Indicator (WRI) in Figure 1-1. Simply circle the letter of the

Figure 1-1. The Work Relationship Indicator—Part I: Personal Assessment.

DESCRIPTORS	NEEDS ASSESSMENT	LEVEL OF INVESTMENT
Circle the letter in the *one* box of descriptors that best describes how you view yourself in your current job.	We all have needs that we are continuously striving to fulfill. Circle the letter in the one box that best reflects your needs at this time.	Circle the letter by the *one* statement that accurately reflects your "level of investment" or commitment to your current organization.
A Neophyte. New to the organization. Experimenting with jobs and roles and trying to find the right one.	**A** Security, social acceptance, approval, shared burden, shared risks, feeling of belonging, in the club, full benefits, stock options, cars, upgraded travel, money, status, insider, sense of history, and connectedness.	**A** My loyalty and commitment to the organization is based on comparable loyalty and commitment to me from the organization.
B "Going steady" with the organization. Testing or looking for a long-term relationship with the organization. Flirting with recruiters but will turn down offers.	**B** Control, respect, inclusion, an alternative to long-term commitment, less emotional attachment and vulnerability, and getting what I've earned.	**B** I am loyal and committed. However, I reserve the right to determine the level of personal sacrifice I'm willing to make for the benefit of the organization.
C Limited partner. Formally engaged to the organization. Chosen for potential inclusion into inner circle. Willing to make some sacrifices.	**C** Mutual commitment, trust, shared risks, part of the club, mentor/sponsor, skills utilized, strengths leveraged, deficits trained out, ability to affect company culture and policy.	**C** I am extremely loyal and very committed. I have sacrificed and/or am willing to sacrifice my personal and social needs for the benefit of my organization.
D Maverick. Opportunistic. In control of relationship—or vulnerable and feel manipulated, used, or restricted.	**D** Skills base, independence, a professional identity, status, beginning rites of passage in the workforce.	**D** I'm committed to learning and doing my job. I feel I'm too new to think of loyalty and commitment in any serious sense right now.
E Full partner. Self-sacrificing. Married to organization. Totally committed for better or worse. Considered an insider. Publicly support the organization.	**E** Financial security, belonging, status, professional validation, dependability, predictability, a solid foundation.	**E** I want to be committed and loyal. Right now I'm trying to figure out what that means to the organization and to me.

box in each column that best describes how you feel now. If you do this exercise before you read on, you'll be guaranteed an unbiased appraisal of your current relationship needs and the investment or commitment you are willing to make to get those needs met. This will be a valuable reference point for determining what you want and where you are going. There are no right or wrong answers.

We'll help you score your assessment at the end of this chapter, but first we introduce you to our Feminine Relationship Model. This model shows how women form relationships personally and professionally and will help you put your own work relationship assessment into perspective.

The Feminine Relationship Model

All relationships go through a natural process of growth and maturation. The Feminine Relationship Model specifies five distinct relationship stages that are distinguished from one another by four factors:

1. How a woman is identified or described within her organization.
2. Particular needs that she is trying to meet.
3. The level of investment and commitment she is willing to make.
4. The organization's agenda for her.

When all factors are considered, a woman's work relationship can be categorized by one of the following stages:

- Stage 1: Dating—playing the field, searching, unattached, neophyte.
- Stage 2: Girlfriend—exclusive commitment, going steady.
- Stage 3A: Mistress—maverick, opportunistic or used, emotionally vulnerable.
- Stage 3B: Fiancée—engaged, limited partner, chosen one.
- Stage 4: Spouse—full partner, married, totally committed and loyal.

We've purposely used these terms to describe work relationships because all women—married or single, heterosexual or homosexual—know what they mean.

Figure 1-2 provides a quick reference chart of the Feminine Relationship Model. Scan this outline to see which of the descriptors, needs, investment/commitment levels, and organizational agendas apply to you in your work relationship.

The Feminine Relationship Development Process

The five stages in a work relationship change as needs and commitments change, but there are three key aspects of relationship building that hold across all patterns of relationship development:

1. *The process is progressive.* Each stage builds on the experience gleaned from the previous stage. Once you enter a stage, you must learn how to get your needs met and be willing to make the investment or commitment necessary to maintain that type of relationship before you can advance to the next stage for development.

2. *You revisit previous stages when you work to establish a new relationship with another individual or organization.* It takes some time for a new relationship to reach the same stage of commitment and investment that you may have had in a previous relationship. For example, once you are married to a company or manager and then get divorced, you will likely have to revisit the Dating, Girlfriend, and Fiancée stages before you get married to a new employer. You will revisit these stages so that both you and your new employer can feel comfortable with your growing commitment to each other. This process of cycling back through the stages typically happens at a faster rate once you've experienced the stages in a previous relationship because you have already learned how to get your needs met at the preceding stage(s).

3. *The process is sequential in the sense that you can't skip stages without doing the work of the previous stage.* If you leave a relationship and begin another one elsewhere, you will hit a roadblock at the same relationship stage where you have unfinished business. Until you complete the development tasks nec-

essary to get your needs met in that stage, you cannot move on to the next one. It is necessary for you to do the hard work and learn the lessons so that you will be free to enter a new relationship without the burden of unfinished business.

We enter into each stage of our work relationship with the hope that our work will contribute positively to our lives. We have assumptions and expectations, and sometimes even anxiety, about what the relationship could hold. To understand how this process works, let's look at one possible scenario from an individual employee's viewpoint. Refer to the flowchart in Figure 1-3. In Chapter 2, we'll examine the relationship from the organization's perspective.

When you begin your career, you seek an employer who appears to understand what you have to offer and seems willing to help you learn what you can become. This is like a dating relationship. You quickly determine whether your initial instincts about what you both have to offer were correct, and if they are, you move to strengthen the relationship. This moves you into the Girlfriend stage.

In return for your agreement to be exclusive to your employer for the time being, you will be rewarded with the benefits of association: a sense of belonging, some measure of dependability in what you can expect of the organization and what it expects of you, status, and an opportunity to develop skills learned in this job so that you earn professional validation. If the relationship continues to be mutually rewarding, one or both parties will look for ways to deepen the commitment.

If both of you believe that the relationship has the potential to last a lifetime, you will segue into the Fiancée stage. In order to enter this stage, though, some sort of formal proposal must be publicly acknowledged by both parties. In work relationships, this formal process of engagement is often couched in the form of a test. You must answer questions such as: Will you relocate? Will you back an unpopular company decision? At the same time, the organization is asking itself: Are you worth the investment? Do the higher-ups in the organization feel that you are a fit for the-

(text continued on page 13)

Figure 1-2. The feminine relationship model.

	STAGE 1 DATING	STAGE 2 GIRLFRIEND	STAGE 3A MISTRESS	STAGE 3B FIANCEE	STAGE 4 SPOUSE
DESCRIPTORS	• Neophyte • Playing the field • New to the organization • Searching • Unattached	• Going steady • Exclusive • First stage commitment • Flattered by other offers, but refuses them	*Deliberate Choice* • Maverick • Opportunistic • In control • Satisfied -OR- *Naive Choice* • Manipulated • Collusive • Used, restricted • Emotionally vulnerable	• Engaged • Limited partner • Chosen one	• Full partner • Married • Total commitment • Loyal to organization • Public face • Insider status
NEEDS	Establish/Re-establish: • Skill base • Independence • Professional identity • Status • Rites of passage • Financial security	• Belonging • Dependability • Status • Professional validation • Predictability • Foundation • Financial security	• Control • Respect and inclusion • Alternative to engagement • Limited expectations • Quasi-committed relationship • Buffered emotions • Earned rewards • Financial security	• Mutual commitment • Trust • Shared risk • Part of the "club" • Mentor/sponsor • Ability to affect company culture and policies • Utilization of skills • Strengths leveraged • Defects trained out • Financial security	• Security • High level of sponsorship • Social acceptance • Approval • Shared burden • Shared risk • Total commitment • Feeling of belonging • In the club • Full benefits • Stock options, bonus • Upgraded perks • Insider status • Sense of history • Financial security

INVESTMENT (COMMITMENT)	• What you do, not who you are • Self focused • Willing to join up and network • Work for financial security • Skill training	• Look at company as "we" • Commitment with limited intimacy • Earnest participation • Financial security • Skill training	• Commitment with limited intimacy • Financial security • Skill base • Training • Forum to utilize skills • Willing to take risks	• Commitment with intimacy • Commitment to long-term relationship • Earnest participation • Forum for perfecting and utilizing skills	• The highest level of investment on a personal, social, and professional basis • Long-term mutual commitment
ORGANIZATION'S AGENDA	• Mutual trial • Training • Orientation/join-up • Safe assignments • Will you fit in? • Will you relocate? • Will you work hard? • Can you handle it?	• Formalization of relationship • Increased opportunities • Mentors and sponsors • Better assignments • Titles • Initiate career pathing	• Loyalty • Push mistress to greater commitment? -OR- Is this relationship to our advantage? • "Family" may try to sabotage mistress • Clandestine support	• Testing of fiancee's loyalty, skills, and fit • Personal interest • Saboteurs can threaten • Celebrate publicly • Scrutinize privately • Increase risk level	• Acceptance of mutual imperfections • Reward with insider information, perks, etc. • Protection • Access to many members of inner circle

Note: It is important to know the meaning of the terms "mentors" and "sponsors" as defined here:

- Mentor: a trusted counselor or guide, a coach, a teacher.
- Sponsor: a person who assumes responsibility for another person's career, a person who pays for or plans and does what is required to make that plan happen (promotion, select job assignment, etc.).

Figure 1-3. The feminine relationship development process.

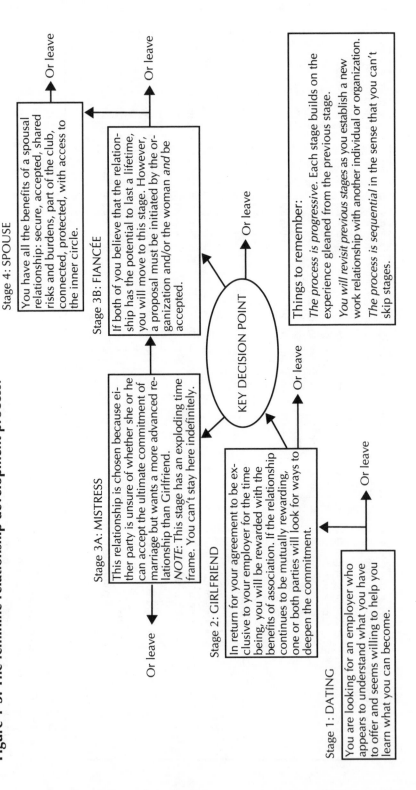

Stage 4: SPOUSE

You have all the benefits of a spousal relationship: secure, accepted, shared risks and burdens, part of the club, connected, protected, with access to the inner circle.

Or leave

Stage 3B: FIANCÉE

If both of you believe that the relationship has the potential to last a lifetime, you will move to this stage. However, a proposal must be initiated by the organization and/or the woman *and* be accepted.

Or leave

Stage 3A: MISTRESS

This relationship is chosen because either party is unsure of whether she or he can accept the ultimate commitment of marriage but wants a more advanced relationship than Girlfriend.
NOTE: This stage has an exploding time frame. You can't stay here indefinitely.

Or leave

KEY DECISION POINT

Or leave

Stage 2: GIRLFRIEND

In return for your agreement to be exclusive to your employer for the time being, you will be rewarded with the benefits of association. If the relationship continues to be mutually rewarding, one or both parties will look for ways to deepen the commitment.

Or leave

Stage 1: DATING

You are looking for an employer who appears to understand what you have to offer and seems willing to help you learn what you can become.

Or leave

Things to remember:
The process is progressive. Each stage builds on the experience gleaned from the previous stage.
You will revisit previous stages as you establish a new work relationship with another individual or organization.
The process is sequential in the sense that you can't skip stages.

will be scrutinizing you while looking for evidence of your commitment and loyalty to them. At the same time, you'll have an opportunity to get a closer look at the organizational family you'll be marrying into. This evaluation is the final determinant of whether you become married to each other. If the answer is yes, you become a spouse of the organization and receive all the benefits of that relationship: You feel secure and accepted, your risks and burdens are shared, you are part of the club with a sense of history and connectedness with the organization.

There is, however, another option: the Mistress stage. This choice can be made deliberately—either party is unsure about pursuing the ultimate commitment of marriage but desires a more advanced relationship than that of Girlfriend—or naively—either party unwittingly falls into a Mistress relationship. The stories in this section describe this phenomenon in greater detail so you can understand how the Mistress stage works. This can be the most confusing and frustrating stage because you have some of the perks of an advanced relationship but not all the public acceptance of your position.

Women and Work: Relationship Tales

Women learn by sharing stories. Ask a woman a yes/no question about someone or something, and you're likely to get a lengthy explanation in place of a one-word answer. That's because women tend to view things in relationship to one another, not in a vacuum. No two situations are ever identical, so it is important for us to understand each one. Review the following tales of professional women in different stages of work relationships. These are true stories; we have disguised the women and their companies in order to ensure confidentiality.

Stage 1: Dating

Joan and the Toads

At age 35, Joan is surprised and frustrated to find herself unemployed and back in the dating game with potential employers. As she spends her days talking with headhunters and gearing up for an onslaught of interviews, she can't help but reflect on the unexpected career journey that has brought her back to this stage.

A graduate from a prestigious university, Joan was pursued by several large companies because of her vibrant personality and remarkable academic record. Despite many competitive offers, Joan was most eager to accept the offer to join the ranks of SalesCo. Immediately, Joan was recognized for her exceptional sales skills and ability to build relationships with important customers. As her reputation for results grew, key male managers within SalesCo began to take notice. She received five promotions in six years and quickly became known as one of two women who had the potential to make it to the top of the sales hierarchy. She was supported within the company, and her results were recognized.

Just when everything seemed to be falling into place, her career hit a snag. She was given a new assignment reporting to a new boss, John. John was clearly a workaholic who valued the input and output of paperwork and a flurry of activity. Joan's style was just the opposite. She measured her success not by the number of orders that came in per month but by the number of long-term customers she had developed. Past managers had rewarded her for this ability, but John became more and more impatient with Joan's style. When he cautioned her about her performance, she was shocked and turned to her previous mentors for support, but no one was in a position to help her. Joan knew that it was time to make a career switch.

She landed a great job with another company in the same field. Once again, she was climbing the ladder of success. Then the same situation occurred: she got a new boss, Steve, with whom she didn't get along. Although there was a lot of private criticism of Steve, no one would challenge him in public—no one except Joan.

Joan's candor was followed by increasingly poor performance reviews. As the relationship between boss and subordinate deteriorated, so did Joan's confidence and self-esteem; having difficulty with managers in both companies raised many self-doubts. Her ultimate decision was to leave the organization in search of a company that would appreciate her strengths.

Joan has now been in a nonstop dating game with companies for several months. Her world revolves around headhunters, résumés, and interviews. She ruminates that she couldn't have chosen a worse time to be unattached to a company because the job market is more competitive than ever.

Armed with records of her past accomplishments, Joan approaches each potential employer with a renewed sense of optimism, but as time passes, she sees her needs becoming more basic. Although ultimately interested in finding a company that she can marry, right now she's just trying to get reestablished. Her needs and willingness to make a commitment are most reflective of those in the Dating stage as outlined in the Feminine Relationship Model in Figure 1-2. She needs to:

✓ Reestablish her professional identity
✓ Gain some financial security and independence
✓ Regain her status
✓ Perhaps build new skills that are more marketable

Joan is not as naive as she was when she first entered this stage fresh out of college fourteen years ago, and it looks as if she is going to have to kiss a lot of toads before she finds her Prince Charming. But she's got her fourth contact with a great company on Wednesday, and things are looking good so far.

Stage 2: Girlfriend

Sharon and Her New Love

Sharon has just found a new love, and it couldn't have happened at a better time. Shocked and confused by the unexpected breakup of her ten-year relationship with the Bright Company, Sharon had been searching for another company where she could again capture the sense of belonging and professional validation she once had.

During her employment at Bright, Sharon had been given increasing responsibility; she was promoted a few levels and was recognized and supported by her managers. Bright was the company she would stay with until she retired.

When Sharon became pregnant with her second child, she followed the same path as she had the first time around: when planning her maternity leave, she made sure that her business was in order and would be handled properly while she was out. Her only concern was that her immediate boss had left the company and had not been replaced yet. In an effort to create a smooth transition, she communicated all of her information to the manager at the next level.

Sharon gave birth to another baby girl, and shortly thereafter returned to work. Immediately, several coworkers approached her about derogatory comments that the new manager, Patricia, had made while she was on maternity leave. Evidently, she had been referring to Sharon as "the Mother" and publicly made comments that "she'll have another child, you wait and see." Sharon felt that Patricia was questioning her commitment to the organization, and Sharon watched as her responsibilities declined. Sharon knew her relationship with Bright had reached a point beyond repair.

Within a few months, Sharon accepted a position with Rescue Research. Already she has gotten signals that her instincts were correct about her new company. The company's culture supports the values that Sharon holds dear: ethics, fair play, open dialogue, encouragement of risk taking, and policies to provide health care and other benefits. She's still trying to get over the loss she feels from no longer being associated with Bright after so many years, but she's beginning to feel as if Rescue could be a company that she could retire with. She still gets calls from recruiters, and although she's flattered by their interest, she forwards them on to other people she knows.

Sharon is in the Girlfriend stage, and she has made a commitment to stick it out for a while to see where the relationship goes. Right now, she's enjoying the attention, along with feelings of:

✓ Belonging
✓ Dependability—they both know what they want from each other for now

✓ Status
✓ Professional validation
✓ Financial security
✓ Predictability

After her breakup with Bright, Sharon is not as eager as she once was to commit herself to a company, but she's not the type to hold back either.

Stage 3A: Mistress

This is the most challenging and complex relationship stage for women. To provide clarity, we'll tell the stories of two women who became mistresses with their organizations under very different circumstances: one as a result of naiveté and one by deliberate choice.

Behind Closed Doors

Sandy had been with the Center for Applied Research for thirteen years. Her career had been an enjoyable adjunct to her personal life, providing her an opportunity to garner accolades for her exceptional technical skills. Sandy had been able to advance her career while also being a wife and mother of three children. She considered herself fortunate: She had a family whom she loved and a secure job with a friendly and supportive boss, Ted.

Then almost suddenly her world changed: Her husband asked her for a divorce. As she struggled through the ending of her marital relationship, she became distracted at work. Ted noticed and began to talk to Sandy about her troubles. Much to Sandy's surprise, Ted understood completely; he was also going through a divorce. Soon they found themselves sharing their stories, talking more and more intimately about their shattered dreams and disappointments and also their hopes and fears about the future. They had always respected each other's business skills; now they had an added dimension to their relationship, and they began spending more and more time together—at work, during lunch hours, and occasionally after work. Although both agreed on the importance of erecting boundaries between their personal and professional lives, they continued to develop a close personal relationship. Ted told Sandy that he had never before had a relationship in which he felt so understood as a man and as a manager. Sandy grew closer to him as well, but although Ted appeared to want more than a friendship, she continued to draw the line: His divorce was not final, he was her boss, and she just didn't feel "right." Ted said he understood and promised to respect her position.

Ted invited her one evening to celebrate his new promotion, and amidst the celebration, Ted gave her a passionate kiss. Sandy reminded him of their promise to refrain from this kind of contact. He smiled at her, and they continued to talk throughout the evening.

After Ted accepted the promotion, their relationship cooled slightly. Ted was moved to another building and became focused on his new position. Shortly after Ted's promotion, a position became available that was perfect for Sandy. It would mean an advancement for her, and Ted would again be her boss. Everyone, including Sandy thought that she would get the job. She didn't. Feeling somewhat betrayed, she scheduled an appointment to talk with Ted about the situation. He appeared warm and friendly but never addressed the reasons why he hadn't picked her for the position. Sandy ultimately determined to preserve her friendship with Ted and ruefully decided that perhaps the job wasn't right for her after all.

She threw herself into her work and successfully moved up a few rungs on the organizational ladder. Then the Center decided to reorganize. A plum position opened up that appeared custom-made for Sandy. As she was interviewing for the job, the players at the top got shuffled, and Ted surfaced as the senior manager in charge. Sandy appeared to be a shoo-in for this prime position: She was the most qualified and also knew the man at the top.

On the advice of a friend, Sandy decided to schedule a meeting with Ted to make sure that their past relationship was not going to interfere with her getting this new position. She and Ted met for lunch off site, and he seemed as warm and kind as ever. He assured her that nothing in their past would affect her career progress. He told Sandy that "things looked good" for her and then asked how her life was going. It almost seemed like old times.

As the time for the job appointments grew nearer, several people congratulated Sandy as the heir apparent. But when the job postings were made, Sandy was shocked to find that she not only didn't get the position she had interviewed for, but her current position had been eliminated in the restructure. She would still be employed at the Center, but it was up to her to find a new position.

Although Sandy has always viewed herself as married to the Center, her current feelings and needs are consistent with those of a naive Mistress:

✓ Striving for respect and inclusion
✓ Buffering her emotions
✓ Wishing she had more control
✓ Trying to get what she thinks she has earned
✓ Feeling used and restricted

In other words, she is desperately searching for an understanding of how her career got derailed. She can't figure out what went wrong.

Sandy's story is not unusual. We've interviewed several women who have learned hard lessons about this perilous stage. Many women fall into the tender trap of becoming too close to a superior only to find that the relationship compromises their career.

Sandy never intended to become a mistress. It is natural for people who work closely together to respond to each other on a personal level, but when intimacy is created between two people at different organizational levels, it can become dangerous, especially for the person who is in the subordinate work relationship, as Sandy is.

Since Sandy had worked hard to erect personal barriers between herself and Ted, she thought she had handled the situation appropriately—and maybe she did. But Ted is now in a position in the company in which his actions are heavily scrutinized, and he has two fears. First, he worries that Sandy could expose his vulnerability; she might share intimate information about him in a way that could embarrass him or jeopardize his position in the company. Second, since others are aware that he and Sandy had a close relationship, they may question his objectivity if he appoints her to a coveted position. Because of these fears, Ted will not grant Sandy the job assignments that she has earned, thereby deliberately placing her in a mistress relationship with the Center. The result? Sandy is stuck in a relationship she neither understands nor wants, and she has a growing animosity for Ted. When she talked to a lawyer friend about the situation, the lawyer became enraged and told her that she should "sue the bastard" for discrimination. Sandy's wondering if that isn't such a bad idea after all.

Despite Sandy's story, the Mistress stage can be a positive one for some women, as the story of Kate, a mistress by deliberate choice, shows.

It's My Party and I'll Do What I Want To—Kate's Story

Kate has almost always been in control. If you're ever in a crisis, she's the one you want to have beside you. She's smart, assertive, and confident, and she knows how to go after what she wants. Sometimes employers who see these traits in a female employee want to run for cover, but not Jim. From the day Kate walked into his office looking for a job, he knew that she had the skills he needed in his company, TechCo. She's been on his payroll for five years now, and he's never been disappointed with her performance.

Kate has been reasonably happy with her career at TechCo. She's been able to build her skills and has been rewarded with promotions and regular pay raises. Sometimes she starts to feel a little unsatisfied but then thinks about how much money she's making and has to smile. Still, over the past two years she has found herself looking for something more rewarding than just making a lot of money. She went to Jim and talked to him about some of the work she could be doing at TechCo. He excitedly told her about a career path he had in mind for her that would continue to advance her up the ladder—heck, she could even take over the company one day!

This prospect didn't thrill Kate as much as it did Jim; in fact, it started to depress her. She realized that she didn't see herself at TechCo over the long term but didn't know what else to do. After thinking about getting an advanced degree that would allow her to move into other fields, she decided to quit TechCo and pursue her M.B.A. degree. Jim couldn't believe it, and he bargained with her to continue working three days a week at TechCo while going to school. He even offered to pay for her classes. He's still hoping that she'll decide to stay with TechCo and help him realize his dreams for the company.

Kate's got other plans. She will continue to work hard at TechCo but after graduation plans to start a consulting business with a classmate. They have already negotiated their first contract.

Kate is clearly a Mistress by deliberate choice. She is:

✓ Opportunistic
✓ In control
✓ Trying to find a successful alternative to marrying the company
✓ Willing to accept the risks of being a Mistress
✓ Putting herself, not TechCo, first
✓ Committed but has limited her intimacy

Kate will probably leave TechCo as soon as she graduates and her plans solidify. Unless something drastic happens, she's already decided that TechCo is not the ultimate work relationship for her. Right now, though, she's calling the shots, and Jim is letting her. Kate's story exemplifies how the Mistress stage can be a successful alternative to a marriage commitment. At this point, both Jim and Kate are happy with their arrangement.

Stage 3B: Fiancée

Let's Take a Look at Janet, Everyone Else Did

As we were contemplating the women we knew who were in Fiancée relationships with their organizations, we were struck by the public brouhaha surrounding Janet Reno's appointment to the position of U.S. attorney general in 1993. Wasn't she going through a very public betrothal to our government and to our commander in chief? Think about it.

Once Reno made the decision to accept President Clinton's appointment of her as attorney general, she entered a Fiancée stage in her career. By accepting Clinton's proposal, she put herself in a position to be examined by every member of America's family. The scrutiny of the first woman in that coveted position was intense.

Although Janet Reno was a chosen one and clearly sponsored and supported by President Clinton, it was up to her to pass the inspection of the public at large. She was given an opportunity to leverage her skills and to affect the culture as it relates to the role of the attorney general in domestic affairs. As the American public was reviewing her record as the state attorney in Miami and probing for revelations of her personal life, she was presented with what was to be her acid test: the Waco disaster. She was held responsible for the combined actions of the FBI and the Alcohol, Tobacco and Firearms (ATF) agents as they struggled to unarm a zealot named David Koresh and his band of followers stationed at an encampment in Waco, Texas.

The standoff between this so-called lamb of God and an army of law enforcement agents became daily fodder for a press-addicted society intent on watching this Fiancée under pressure. Ultimately an order was given to storm Koresh's compound and seize the weapons. In the ensuing attack, the compound was set ablaze, and many of Koresh's followers, including women and children, lost their lives. As critics reviled the decision, Reno stood ready to shoulder the burden of the disaster. By offering to resign her position, in a gesture similar to giving back an engagement ring, she showed her ultimate readiness to sacrifice herself for her country if that were to be the outcome. Finally, it was her courageous participation in a House Judiciary Committee hearing that ultimately won her the respect of a nation. As evidence, we present *Time* magazine's account of this scenario:

> It is her performance under pressure that has sealed her stature in the capital. During a House Judiciary Committee hearing on the Waco disaster, Reno found

herself under fire from [a] Congressman [who challenged], "You did the right thing by offering to resign. And now I'd like you to know that there is at least one member of Congress that isn't going to rationalize the death of two dozen children."

[Reno's] voice quavering, she replied, "I haven't tried to rationalize the death of children, Congressman. I feel more strongly about it than you will ever know. But I have neither tried to rationalize the death of four agents, and I will not walk away from a compound where ATF agents had been killed by people who knew they were agents and leave them unsurrounded." Then she added, "Most of all, Congressman, I will not engage in recrimination."

In that instant, Reno, who had already pretty much captivated Washington with one gutsy performance after another, achieved full-fledged folk-hero status. . . . At present, the praise is all but unanimous.[1]

Janet Reno's story is clear evidence that the process of relationship development is sequential; you can't skip stages. She had to endure intense scrutiny from the American public in this stage as her marriage potential was evaluated. At this point, we have witnessed the following signs indicative of her Fiancée status:

- ✓ Mutual commitment
- ✓ Trust
- ✓ Shared risk
- ✓ Sponsorship
- ✓ Utilization of skills
- ✓ Strengths leveraged, deficits trained out
- ✓ Earnest participation
- ✓ Forum for perfecting and utilizing skills
- ✓ Loyalty, skills, and fit with the organization tested

Stage 4: Marriage

Good Things Come to Those Who Wait, Right Betty?

Betty is the type of woman who gets married once and stays married—forever and ever, amen. That is what she was taught to believe growing up, and it is what she still believes today. Early on, her parents imbued her with a respect for qualities such as loyalty, commitment, trust, and a strong belief in family. Since she grew up in a family environment that operated under principles of fairness, truthfulness, and self-confidence, she finds it hard to believe that anyone could have different principles of conduct. She is naturally optimistic, always choosing to believe the best about people and situations. And she possesses a high energy level that supports her desires to be an accomplished wife, mother, and career woman.

When Betty sets her sights on something, she zealously pursues it until she gets it. That's the way that she approached her marriage to her husband, Harry, and that's the way she has approached her lifelong career at the Health Care Organization (HCO). From the moment that her dress heels first clicked across the terrazzo at HCO's headquarters, she knew that this would be the company she would share her professional life with. She had memorized all the company brochures they had sent to her prior to that first interview, and she was especially pleased with what she read about HCO's belief that people were the organization's strongest business asset.

HCO was equally impressed with Betty. Everyone who met her noted her optimistic determination and sincere commitment to helping provide superior health care to the clients HCO served. They enthusiastically offered her a job and talked freely about the positions she could aspire to within HCO. They operated their company like a family, taking care of individual needs by offering generous health benefits and rewarding loyal service with profit-sharing and bonus plans. This was music to Betty's ears, and she accepted the job on the spot.

Betty's career with HCO became an integral part of her life. She believed wholeheartedly in the company and worked diligently to advance her position. Harry was supportive, particularly when it came to being an active father for their two children. Betty thought she was doing a pretty good job of balancing her home and work life, but after several years, it was beginning to wear on her. Although she had always been an avid cheerleader for the company line, she was beginning to consider her own needs.

When HCO decided to restructure the organization, Betty saw it as an opportunity to request a position that would allow her to spend more time with her family. HCO asked employees to outline their requests, and Betty indicated that she wanted to limit her travel time. Since she had been a top-rated and loyal performer, she expected that her request would be granted.

The new assignments were made, and Betty was surprised to see that she was given an assignment requiring travel almost weekly. But she believed in the company, and saw this as a test of her loyalty and commitment. She talked with her sponsor, Jerry, about it, and he assured her that she would be taken care of in the long run. He mentioned that the company was changing, and they needed her skills in this particular job for the time being; if she would help them out now, he would make sure that she got what she wanted later.

Betty wasn't the only one displeased with the new assignments. Almost everyone seemed to be grousing about the changes the company was making and how the company didn't seem to care about people anymore. Betty began to witness some pretty poor treatment of employees, but she rationalized that there must be something behind these actions that she didn't know about. Nothing was going to shake her confidence in HCO. She continued to be an optimistic cheerleader for the company and refrained from the destructive banter that seemed to be constantly buzzing throughout the halls of her company. She concentrated on improving her skills and her contribution to the organization.

Over the next few years, Betty was on the road a lot, racing home whenever she could to watch her son get another belt in karate or her daughter perform in a piano recital. Her husband, Harry, continued to be supportive. Then HCO went through another big downsizing, and everyone became fearful of losing their jobs. Betty hoped that this time her sponsor, Jerry, would indeed take care of her. Although she knew that there would be large cutbacks, she dared to hope that she would receive one of the prime appointments, one where she could work in the same city and limit her travel. After all, she had made the sacrifices, remained loyal to the company, never bad-mouthed decisions, never engaged in negativity. She had done whatever she was asked to do, and had done it without question.

On the big day when the appointments were announced, Betty was ecstatic to learn that she had gotten one of the prime jobs. Her coworkers inquired behind her back why she was chosen, but the reason is clear: Betty had proved herself to have all the qualities the company was looking for in a spouse. Not only did she have a strong track record, but she had also:

✓ Invested and committed herself at the highest level possible personally and professionally
✓ Acted as if she were married to the organization
✓ Proved her total commitment despite personal sacrifice
✓ Always showed her public approval of the company
✓ Had a sponsor high in the organization

Her appointment to this key position sent a message to the rest of the organization: It heralded the company's strong endorsement of her and it proved that good things come to those who wait. Betty has successfully navigated through all the stages to earn herself a position as a protected spouse in this organization.

Summary Exercise

By now you should have a good understanding of how the five relationship stages are played out in organizations. You can see how we pursue relationships with our organizations for reasons that are unique to each of us. These relationships don't always work out as planned; sometimes we progress quickly through the stages, sometimes we hit roadblocks, and sometimes we go back through the stages when our relationships end and begin anew elsewhere. How do these concepts play out with the people you know? Take a moment to assess the work relationships of the people you know and the reasons why you think they are in that stage:

People I know who are Dating: because:

_____   _____

_____   _____

People I know who are   because:

Girlfriends:———————   _____

_____   _____

People I know who are   because:

Mistresses: ———————   _____

_____   _____

People I know who are   because:

Fiancées:———————   _____

_____   _____

People I know who are   because:

Spouses: ———————   _____

_____   _____

Now that you understand the feminine relationship development process, look at your own assessment of your work relationship that you completed in Figure 1-1.

Go back and look at the selection you made for each of the three indicators, and use the following key to identify the stage that corresponds to the letters you circled in each column:

Descriptors	*Needs Assessment*	*Level of Investment*
A = Dating	A = Marriage	A = Mistress
B = Girlfriend	B = Mistress	B = Fiancée
C = Fiancée	C = Fiancée	C = Marriage
D = Mistress	D = Dating	D = Dating
E = Marriage	E = Girlfriend	E = Girlfriend

Now write down the relationship stage that you assessed in each of the three categories:

Descriptors   Needs Assessment   Level of Investment

Stage: _____   _____   _____

If you indicated the same stage in all three categories, that's the *definite* relationship stage you believe you have with your organization. If you indicated the same stage in two of the three categories, that's the *dominant* relationship stage you believe you have with your organization. If there are no similarities, you are in a *transition* stage.

If you are comfortable with your assessment . . . If you feel that the assessment is on target and are comfortable with it, your next step is to see if your organization is viewing your relationship in the same way. Once you have an accurate picture of your relationship with your employer, you can begin to contemplate where you want to go next. You may simply want to make sure that you are able to maintain what you've got, you may want to advance, or you may decide to retreat a stage. The next chapter will help you understand what the organization's agenda will be for you in any relationship stage.

If you are getting mixed signals from your relationship . . . Mixed signals are an indicator that you are between stages. Keep in mind that your needs aren't static, and neither are your relationships. You may want to review the descriptors, needs, and investments outlined in Figure 1-2. Chapter 2 will give you a broader understanding that will help you clarify the relationship stage you are really in.

Where Are You Now? A Journal Opportunity

In workshops we've conducted, we've found that writing a journal is an excellent tool for clarifying thoughts. You are engaged in a personal process of evaluating a relationship of significance in your life. As you make your way through it, questions will surface, issues will become clearer, and you'll get a more distinct picture of the reality you are living. Jot down your feelings as you experience them, and you will have a reference point for making future choices. To get you started, we've posed a few questions for you to consider:

My own personal assessment is that I am in a ———————— stage relationship.

This is [   ] the same or [   ] different from where I thought I was prior to reading this chapter because:————————————
————————————————————————————.

I'm looking for a ————————————stage relationship because: ————————————————————————
————————————————————————————.

My reactions to what I've learned about my relationship stage are:————————————————————————————
————————————————————————————.

Things I want to think about are:————————————————
————————————————————————————.

2

Relationships Take Two

Humans must breathe, but corporations must make money.
Alice Embee, in *Meditations for Women Who Do Too Much*

There are two sides to every relationship. In this chapter you will examine your work relationship from your employer's perspective based on the company's needs and level of investment in you. You'll determine whether the signals your managers are sending you are indicative of the relationship you believe you have with them. You can then ask yourself where you think the relationship is headed and if you are willing to make choices consistent with the needs the organization has of you at a particular stage. In short, this chapter is a reality check to help you understand both sides of the relationship and see if you and your organization are seeing eye to eye. If you're not, you're probably already experiencing signs of stress because of misaligned expectations.

Organizations Have Needs, Too

Organizations foster relationships with their employees in an effort to get their needs met, especially their primary need: to make a profit. The methods they employ to get that profit depend on their culture or the current power elite, but in general, two types of cultures exist relative to the treatment of employees: up-or-out or family loyalty.

In the up-or-out culture, the organization provides clarity on the objectives it needs to accomplish. Individuals are recruited, trained, and evaluated on their ability to meet those objectives. The focus is on high productivity, and you are either promoted up the hierarchy by receiving more responsibility, or you are counseled out of the organization due to lack of performance. In this culture, the organization will try to help you meet your needs as long as that assistance can be directly correlated to helping you achieve the organization's objectives. The organization views your relationship as a means to getting work done, and its interest is primarily in what you do, not how you feel.

Loyalty-oriented organizations, on the other hand, believe that their greatest asset is the loyalty, commitment, and dedication of their employees. They strive to create a familial environment in which people feel good about being part of a team. Promotions are typically made from within the company, giving employees a home team advantage. Additionally, these organizations strive to offer their employees exceptional benefit packages as an incentive for dedicated service.

A friendly warning: A company's culture gives you a clue about how it is likely to approach a relationship with you. But the important thing to remember is that regardless of whether the culture is up or out or loyalty oriented, the organization's very existence is dependent on its ability to make a profit. This need supersedes any needs that you may have. In today's difficult economic climate, we've begun to see more and more companies shift from a loyalty-oriented culture to an up-or-out one. Witness recent massive layoffs at companies like IBM, Boeing, and Procter & Gamble. When push comes to shove, an organization's primary responsibility is to its shareholders, and as a result, your personal needs are secondary at best.

The Organization's Agenda

Organizations follow patterns of relationship development in much the same way as you pursue a relationship with them.

Their approach is similar to the stages concept in that it is a progressive development advancing you up the hierarchy as you learn and apply skills, become more savvy, produce increasing results, and become more committed. Our experience is that companies are comfortable dealing with women along the relationship continuum that women naturally follow.

Since the majority of larger organizations are owned and operated by males, they have experience dealing with women in the various relationship situations we described in Chapter 1. They understand that you have different needs at different stages in your relationship, and they are willing to help you get your needs met as long as you are helping them get theirs met as well. This translates into an organizational agenda with signals and tests administered as milestones for advancing through the relationship stages from Dating to Marriage. By seeing how companies operate in each relationship stage, you'll be able to make connections with behaviors that you have witnessed but perhaps not understood. Figure 2-1 is a quick reference guide to these signals and tests.

Stage 1: Dating

In this stage the organization is making two assessments:

1. Are you a good match for the culture in terms of work ethic, philosophy, personality, and other characteristics?
2. Do you possess the required skills and abilities, and are you trainable? The organization's investment is limited to this agenda, and as a result it will most likely signal a woman in the Dating stage by offering some or all of the following:

✓ Orientation to the company culture
✓ Initial skill assessment and training
✓ Safe assignments, limited responsibility, limited autonomy
✓ A big picture view of career possibilities and a vague career path
✓ Possible payment for the cost of relocation if required
✓ Promise of benefits if the relationship lasts longer than

Figure 2-1. The organization's agenda.

STAGE 1: DATING	STAGE 2: GIRLFRIEND	STAGE 3A: MISTRESS	STAGE 3B: FIANCÉE	STAGE 4: SPOUSE
• Mutual trial • Training • Orientation • Safe assignments • Determination of organizational fit: Will you fit in? Will you relocate? Will you work hard? Can you handle it?	• Formalization of relationship • Increased opportunities • Mentors and sponsors* • Better assignments • Titles • Career pathing	• Loyalty • Test of relationship • Possible sabotage by "family" • Clandestine support	• Testing of loyalty • Personal interest • Threat of career saboteurs • Public acknowledgment • Private scrutiny • Increased risk	• Acceptance of mutual imperfections • Rewards: insider information, perks, etc. • Protection • Access to many members of inner circle

*A *mentor* is a trusted counselor or guide, a coach, a teacher. A *sponsor* is a person who assumes responsibility for another person's career; a person who pays for or plans and does what is required to make that plan happen (promotion, select job assignment, etc.).

six months, with increasing benefits consistent with loyalty and longevity
✓ Possible signing bonus if you were aggressively recruited from another organization

This is viewed as an initial trial stage for both parties. As soon as you can prove that you fit and your skills are a match, you can advance to the Girlfriend stage, just as Sharon did at Rescue Research in Chapter 1.

Stage 2: Girlfriend

Your relationship has been established and acknowledged. Now the organization wants answers to two questions:

1. Will you continue to grow and contribute to the accomplishment of the organization's objectives?
2. Will that growth lead to a deeper commitment from both parties?

The organization's management will signal that they are committed to you at this stage in the following ways:

✓ Increased opportunities for you to display your skills and savvy:
　—Through assignments of complex tasks that can distinguish you from your peers
　—Via an opportunity to work with a team of respected colleagues, some in positions above yours in the hierarchy
　—Via an opportunity to make a presentation to key individuals
✓ Mentors and sponsors to assist you in plotting a career path
✓ Promotions as a reward for your proved performance

As your performance continues to improve, the organization's interest in you will increase. Important to note is the appearance of mentors and sponsors. For clarification, a *mentor* is someone whom you trust to give you coaching and guidance. A *sponsor* is someone who has the power and ability to influence and actually make things happen in your work relationship with your organization.

Now you have the opportunity to advance your career via two options: you can become a Fiancée or a Mistress.

Stage 3A: Mistress

The organization's agenda varies depending on whether you are a mistress by deliberate or naive choice. Let's look at each situation.

Mistress by Deliberate Choice

In this situation, the company wants to marry you; you are trying to find a successful alternative to becoming a Fiancée, although you want a more advanced relationship than you had in the Girlfriend stage. The caveat is that you will not receive the public accolades and acknowledgments awarded to a Fiancée because you have not committed yourself, and the organization knows it.

It is rare for a woman to remain a Mistress for her entire career. For example, she may realize that she has gotten all she can out of the relationship and must forge a new relationship elsewhere in order to get her needs met. Or her sponsor finds that he or she cannot protect her any longer and she is forced out of the organization. Or she finds that she can't withstand the pressure from others in the organization. That is why we warn you that this stage has an exploding time frame. The relationship pressure in this stage is greater than in any other stage.

Mistress by Naive Choice

You can be swept into this stage unknowingly when either the organization or your sponsor determines that their needs would be best met by placing you in this stage. Either may think that you don't have the requisite skills or personal style to merit an official proposal for a long-term commitment, but they want to continue to take advantage of your current relationship and skills. If you are caught in this dilemma, you are probably frustrated, confused, and anxious; you sense that your position is being compromised, but you're not sure where your relationship stands. Or you may be in denial, choosing to believe that your sponsor or organization is sending you signals that marriage is in the cards. If your sponsor's relationship with the organization changes or if there is a shift in the reins of power, you could be sacrificed.

Let's look at Sandy's story again. Although she never intended to become a Mistress in her company, her personal relationship with a powerful sponsor compromised her ability to become married to the organization. Once Ted had made himself vulnerable to her by sharing his innermost feelings, he was not about to allow her a position where she could use that knowledge against him. Yet from Sandy's perspective, she believed that the sharing meant that he, as a representative of the company, was intending to marry her. Instead, he got his needs met at her expense, and his refusal to assign her to a valued position has tarnished her reputation within the company. She is stuck in a Mistress dilemma.

The organization will ask the following questions in this stage if you deliberately choose Mistress:

1. Will you ever make a public, exclusive commitment to us?
2. Will your reluctance to make that commitment challenge our relationships with others who are committed to the family?

If you naively choose Mistress, these are the questions:

1. Can we capitalize on your unique skills and abilities to get our organizational objectives met without having to make a long-term commitment to you?
2. Can we offer you enough extras to entice you to stay but not inflame those who are part of the inner circle?

If the organization agrees to enter into this type of relationship with you, you can expect to receive some or all of the following signals:

- ✓ Select exposure to the power elite controlled by your mentors/sponsors and supervisors
- ✓ Continued skill training but probably not a promotion or upgraded title
- ✓ Clandestine support relationships, with private accolades but no public recognition
- ✓ Assignments that leverage your unique skills and abilities without advancing you hierarchically
- ✓ Increased scrutiny and pressure from people who have a Fiancée or Spouse relationship with the organization. (They've made the commitment, why can't you?)
- ✓ Promises of future commitments from the individual or the organization

Almost all of the women we interviewed who were in the Mistress stage ultimately left their organizations. The Mistresses who left under the best circumstances were those who came to terms with the fact that either they or their organization would never be able to make the long-term commitment necessary to advance past this stage.

However, in some rare cases, women have ultimately made the shift from mistress to spouse. In order to make this relationship change, women must first become a fiancée.

Stage 3B: Fiancée

Once the company has issued the proposal and you have accepted, the real testing begins. The questions the organization has are these:

1. Given the exposure, will you meet the expectations of the company family? That is, are your personal politics, ethics, and operating principles consistent with those of the organization? Does your personal life (children, dual career, life-style compatibility) present any barriers or

threats to your company loyalty? Are other Spouses in
the organization comfortable with you?

2. Will you make a public admission of loyalty to the organization—for example, by relocating even though you or
your family doesn't want to, publicly supporting an unpopular company decision, covering for a lie or indiscre-
tion made by the company, merging your identity with
that of the organization, accepting an unappealing job assignment if requested to, or distancing yourself from your
relationships with those who are lower in the hierarchy

As you establish your loyalty and compatibility, you will
receive some or all of these signals:

✓ Mutual trust and shared risks
✓ Increased mentorship and sponsorship
✓ More intimate exposure to the inner circle or power elite
via lunches, dinners, parties, and meetings
✓ Insider information on how the organization really func-
tions and the roles various individuals play
✓ Advanced skill training to correct your own shortcomings
✓ Forum for leveraging existing skills and rewards for
doing so
✓ Public acknowledgment and celebration of your suc-
cesses
✓ Beginning opportunity to influence and affect company
culture and policy
✓ Trust

When these milestones have been achieved, you are ready
to cement your relationship by becoming a Spouse.

Stage 4: Spouse

At this point you have been tested and approved. Only one
question remains:

• Can you maintain the day-in and day-out commitment of
the relationship?

The company now supports your ongoing commitment in the form of these signals:

✓ Full perks, including possible stock options, upgraded travel, generous expense account, full health coverage, greater pay, bonuses
✓ Acceptance of your imperfections
✓ High level of sponsorship
✓ Insider status
✓ Financial security
✓ Shared risks and shared burdens
✓ Total commitment
✓ Feeling of belonging and of being "in the club"
✓ Sense of history and connectedness

In the past, you were guaranteed a career for life once you achieved Spouse status. The only thing that could bump you from this haven was if you publicly violated the marriage contract in some way (publicly embarrassing the company, for example, or cheating it). In today's competitive world, however, even CEOs are no longer as protected as they once were.

So, How Does Your Organization See You?

To determine how your organization views your relationship, take the Work Relationship Indicator—Part II: Company Signals now (Figure 2-2).

Figure 2-2. The Work Relationship Indicator—Part II: Company Signals.

Directions: The way your company relates to you is often communicated through events, nonverbal signals, or feelings you sense. Check if you have received any of the following signals from your organization in the past two years.

In the last year or two . . .

A _____ 1. My organization has given me safe assignments because I'm new.
B _____ 2. I received my first company pin for length of service.

(continued)

Figure 2-2. Continued.

C ——   3. The organization publicly recognized my contributions.
D ——   4. I get private, not public, accolades for my performance.
E ——   5. The change in the reins of power did not affect my position.
A ——   6. My organization provided me training to ensure I got started successfully.
B ——   7. I received my first promotion sooner than expected.
C ——   8. Others have tried to sabotage my relationships with key hierarchy.
D ——   9. I've received contradictory feedback—my performance is good, but I don't seem to fit in.
E ——   10. The organization required me to put its priorities before my own.
A ——   11. I have not been given total freedom to execute projects assigned to me.
B ——   12. I have been sponsored by the right people who make things happen.
C ——   13. Key people at work have invited me to their social affairs.
D ——   14. My organization gives me mixed signals about its commitment to me.
E ——   15. I was included in the executive compensation and bonus plan.
A ——   16. My organization has given me limited responsibility on the job.
B ——   17. I got a better job title but not increased responsibilities or compensation.
C ——   18. The risks to the organization, for my decisions, have increased significantly.
D ——   19. The organization wants me to make a long-term commitment.
E ——   20. It's been like a marriage: the company is comfortable with my strengths and imperfections.
A ——   21. My organization has shared its big picture for my career potential.
B ——   22. I had a career discussion confirming the organization's commitment to me.
C ——   23. My identity has evolved to what's expected at my level.
D ——   24. I noticed that I got the perks but not the title.
E ——   25. I still am or have become part of the inner circle and power elite of our organization.

To derive your score, count the number of checks you had for each letter A–E and place the number by each letter below:

A____   B____   C____   D____   E____
(= Dating) (= Girlfriend) (= Fiancée) (= Mistress) (= Spouse)

The number of checks in each category indicates the type of relationship your company thinks you have with it:

- Five or more checks indicate a *definite* relationship
- Three to four checks indicate a *dominant* relationship; you may be moving toward or away from this relationship stage.
- One to three checks indicate the *transition* stage. You are getting mixed signals from your organization, or you are in transition between stages in your work relationship.

Compare this evaluation with the personal assessment you made of your relationship in Chapter 1:

My assessment of   Organization's assessment

my work relationship   of our work relationship

_____   _____

Consistent?
Yes_____   No_____ Partially_____

If the evaluations are exactly the same, then you and your organization have a common perspective of the relationship. This is your *definite* work relationship at present. If the evaluations are partially consistent, then a *dominant* relationship stage is indicated. In either case, you and the organization are both operating at the same stage, so you'll both be more likely to get your needs met mutually. Your next step is to determine whether this is the best relationship for you now and in the future.

If there is any inconsistency in how your relationship is viewed, two scenarios are possible:

1. You'll be disappointed by unmet needs because your expectations of the organization are greater than what it is

prepared to give you. You may not be reading the signals it is sending you.

2. Your organization will be disappointed because it doesn't understand your needs and aspirations. Perhaps there is information you have withheld from it intentionally or unintentionally.

Let's look at the first scenario, where you may be disappointed by unmet needs. If your own evaluation places you in a stage more advanced than the one indicated by your company signals, then you need to reevaluate the situation. In the case of Sandy and the Center for Applied Research outlined in Chapter 1, Sandy felt certain that she was married to the organization. It wasn't until she was passed over for two important assignments that she came to the painful realization that she was considered a Mistress by the power elite. She may have missed the following signals:

- Getting private, not public, accolades for her performance
- Receiving contradictory feedback (her performance is good, but she doesn't seem to fit in)
- Noticing that she got the perks but not the title

If, on the other hand, the signals from your organization indicate that it views your relationship as more advanced than you perceive, then you may be holding back something. Perhaps you haven't determined whether you are willing to make the long-term commitment required to advance toward the Spouse stage. Or you may be between stages, but not yet ready to move on.

What Have You Learned? A Journal Opportunity

Congratulations on completing this first step in understanding the complexities of your work relationship. You should now be able to answer the following questions:

What is my work relationship about anyway? What needs have I been trying to get met, and what commitments am I willing to make?

_____

_____

_____

Has there been a difference in how my organization views my work relationship and how I see it? Why? What's been missed?

_____

_____

_____

_____

_____

Right now I'm feeling _____about my work relationship because_____.

_____

_____

_____

In Part II, you'll have a chance to take a closer look at the dynamics of your work relationship and its effect on you personally.

Part II
Trouble in
Paradise?

Nothing in life is to be feared. It is only to be understood.
Madame Curie, in *Great Quotes from Great Women*

The exercises in Part I were designed to help you understand the work relationship you have with your organization. You may have realized that what you want and need does not match what the organization wants and needs, an incongruity that can be a source of tremendous stress. Or you may have found that you don't have the relationship with the organization that you desire. Perhaps you aspire to be a Spouse, with all of the benefits of that relationship, but find that you are a Mistress involved in a relationship of mutual convenience. Maybe you're stuck in the Dating stage, hopping from job to job, not being able to start the commitment process. Worse, maybe you're experiencing multiple rejections from companies that only want to go to the Fiancée stage and not commit any further. Do you feel like the bridesmaid but never the bride?

Even when we know our relationships aren't what we want, it's difficult to think they may end. For the moment, it's all we have and all we know. Nonetheless, we experience a range of emotions that must be dealt with sooner or later.

Part II is designed to help you identify if there's trouble in your relationship and how this relationship is affecting the three spheres of your life: personal, social, and work. In Chapter 3 we identify common warning signs of a troubled relationship, offer a checklist that assesses how prevalent these warnings are in your work relationship, identify potential emotional reactions, and present case studies that illustrate the interconnectedness of the warning signs and your emotional reactions.

Chapter 4 explores the concept of the three spheres of your life—personal social, work—within the context of your mental pictures and your realities. We also assist you in "hearing" the kinds of messages you may be receiving but not listening to. A quiz helps you assess if there is a high level of concerned messages in any or all of the three major spheres of your life. The chapter closes by helping you integrate all of the information you've learned so you will be prepared to begin the process of creating a work relationship that's best for you.

3

Is Your Work Relationship at Risk?

[Work] relationships should enhance our lives and although at best they include unpleasant experiences, when the majority of the experiences are unpleasant, then questions about the viability of the relationship need to be raised.

Daphne Rose Kingma, *Coming Apart—Why Relationships End and How to Live Through the Ending of Yours*

Women have come a long way in a relatively short period of time. The sheer numbers of women entering the workforce since 1970, particularly in management and professional positions, is staggering. We know how to interview for that job and get it, and we're dealing with hurdles that confront us daily. A lot has changed since that first generation of women broke new ground into nontraditional careers such as engineering, science, and medicine. These women endured ridicule and ostracization, and they suffered negative stereotypes to get that coveted degree. Others delayed or sacrificed having children because their work relationships were so demanding and consuming that the time was never quite right. And then there were those who decided to be superwomen. They had a work relationship that was exhausting, children who needed attention, and a husband or lover who stood in line as the last priority. These women moved too many times to count, took the fifteenth trip in one month, and yet stayed committed to their work relationship.

Women want work to matter, and to be fulfilling for a lifetime. We want to be treated fairly, respected, and valued, with all the rights and privileges commensurate with the investments we make. We expect reciprocal commitments because of the high price we have paid to be in these relationships. We learned that there were a lot of things that we could control in our work relationships, and yet there are some things we have no influence over at all.

What happens when you start getting those feelings of trouble in paradise—that something isn't quite right with your work relationship? Your emotions may range from utter confusion to feeling as if you're on an emotional roller coaster. Part of the confusion may be that relationships are not good all the time; you may get a poor supervisor, an undesirable assignment, or irritable colleagues. In these situations, you're careful not to overreact to what may prove to be a temporary situation.

But you may also be dealing with such monumental issues as continual confrontations, running into brick wall after brick wall and broken promises again and again, stress, still being an outsider. When the trouble becomes unmanageable, you experience many thoughts and feelings. You may feel guilty for having confused and angry thoughts since so many people have told you how fortunate and special you are to have achieved so much. You think, "What an honor and privilege to have been chosen by this organization. I'm making more money than I ever dreamed of. How can I be so ungrateful! How can I explain a troubled work relationship to my parents, friends, children, lover or husband?" You feel lonely and misunderstood because you can't communicate what you don't understand. So you spend months suffering in silence or dragging others down with you. You try to figure out what's wrong, try to fix it, try to fix yourself, and do whatever you can think of to make it work. Over time, you begin to feel as if you're on a merry-go-round you can't get off. How can you start to make things right again?

This chapter is designed to help you jump off the merry-go-round. First, we take a hard look at the warning signs you may be experiencing in your work relationship. Then we examine the types of emotional reactions you may encounter as your awareness of trouble in paradise begins to grow. There are two sides to every relationship, so you'll also be challenged to examine emotional reactions from the organization. So, let's jump right in to see which, if any, warning signs may apply to you.

TROUBLE IN PARADISE

Checklist of Common Warning Signs

This list represents some common warning signs that indicate trouble in your work relationship. Check those that apply to you.

- ☐ People at work are sending me weird messages. They ignore me and sometimes don't include me. This makes me angry.

- ☐ Everything's a fight. I feel as if I'm at war. Every day I feel as if I have to put on a coat of armor before going to work.

- ☐ I've been thinking about flirting with a headhunter lately. Another job seems like the way out. I need to feel valued.

- ☐ I find myself daydreaming about what my life would be like without this work relationship, without this job.

- ☐ I'm completely disinterested in this job, the company, my work relationship. If it works out, fine; if it doesn't, that's okay.

- ☐ I wonder if this is all there is? Is this what I've spent my life preparing for?

- ☐ Sometimes I feel as if I'm losing it. I'm not sleeping well. And when I do, I have nightmares about work.

- ☐ It seems as if I'm always sick. Even being sick is a relief because it's an excuse not to go to work.

- ☐ I don't trust anyone at work or anything they say.

- ☐ Work is no fun anymore. I've lost my passion for it.

If you checked seven or more signs, there may be significant difficulties in your work relationship, and it's at risk. If you have checked four to six signs, you're approaching major problems in your relationship. If you checked three or fewer, you may just be experiencing a momentarily difficult period.

Emotional Reactions to Trouble in Paradise

Your Emotional Reactions

The warning signs in the preceding checklist represent the craziness, paranoia, hurt, anger, and loneliness commonly experienced by most women when their work relationships are falling apart. In fact, your emotional reactions to a failing work relationship feel very similar to those when a love relationship is breaking up. You feel dejected, confused, and cheated. You've invested your energies to make the relationship work, and this is the payoff: an unfulfilling and uncommitted work relationship.

In interviewing women about their troubled work relationships, we have found that their reactions intensified as the duration of the trouble increased. For many women, this trouble went on so long that it seemed as if nothing could improve it, and they lost hope. Many opted to divorce their work relationships. Shanteil, a woman we interviewed, referred to the relationship as "a treadmill gone out of control. Things just kept getting worse until all balance was lost, and I fell off the treadmill on my rear end." Unfortunately for Shanteil, she hasn't been able to move past the pain and anguish: "I'm just starting to get over it after three years. It's funny how the memories of that experience overshadowed any joy I felt starting new work relationships with new companies. My sad feelings and anger kept making it difficult for me to give my all to a new work relationship. So in three years, I've left two companies because I just couldn't make it work."

Other women we interviewed got stuck experiencing one particularly overwhelming emotional reaction. Joanne described her final year as one of continual torment and confrontation: "Every week I was in some type of confrontation, until things got to the point where I just quit and walked out!" Because she opted out, there was no opportunity for Joanne's work relationship to go progressively through the rest of the process, known as uncoupling, which explains the emotional reactions experienced when personal or work relationships end. We've adapted this process by specifying six distinct stages characterized by six emotional reactions: Distancing, Disengaging, Confronting, Acknowledging, Fix It—Make It Right, and Ending It.

This emotional uncoupling process works in two ways. First, it can be linear and progressive. For example, if a problem is not resolved in a previous stage, it gets progressively worse as the relationship moves through the remaining stages, and eventually, the relationship ends. Second, the relationship becomes so intense at a particular stage that it terminates in that stage.

The Organization's Emotional Reactions

The organization may also be experiencing a myriad of emotional reactions, and it may become difficult to determine if your reactions were triggered by the organization or the organization is responding to you. This is true in our personal relationships too. The trouble gets so interwoven that it's hard to determine how it got started.

Keep in mind that when issues remain unresolved at a particular stage, the organization is also searching for the next step: Will it work with you during this difficult period or contemplate divorce? The more intense the trouble is in the work relationship, the more people and systems (informal and formal) the organization will bring together to paint a "problem" picture of you to validate its position. This is often called "building a file" or "building a case" and contributes to your feelings of being outnumbered and helpless. When the organization has decided to divorce you, it starts asking others to take sides and sometimes overtly shun you.

The organization's proclivity to stack the cards against you is grounded in its culture, how it values employees, the current business climate, and you. Thus, it becomes critical that you not only understand your own emotional reactions but those of the organization. We know this is very difficult to do when you're trying to understand and manage your own emotional reactions, but you must get some distance from your own pain and comprehend what your organization is feeling and how it is reacting to you. Figure 3-1 (on pages 54–55) sets out the information you need to make clear choices.

This uncoupling process represents the second core premise of *Smart Women, Smart Moves*: Women experience similar emotional reactions to a troubled work and personal relationship. This book will help you navigate through these reactions while remaining in control so that you make the best choices for yourself. This choice is not always to leave your work relationship. If you can acknowledge there's a problem in your work relationship, identify the issues, and work through these challenges, then your relationship may be saved and improved significantly—at least enough for you to want to stay. The rest of Chapter 3 is designed to help assess the intensity of trouble in your relationship.

Case Studies

Both of us have felt the anguish of a work relationship gone awry and know that when you're in the midst of a disintegrating relationship, it is natural to feel overwhelmed, out of control, and alone. You may think things will never get better and that a failed work relationship portends a failed career, but that doesn't have to be the case. You will get through this period and will be stronger for having faced these difficulties, as the following stories will show.

Flirting: The Dance with the Headhunters/ Daydreaming

Recently, Marian had become increasingly tempted to talk with headhunters to pursue some of the enticing opportunities they had mentioned. She was surprised that she would even consider leaving her job but realized how much her work situation had changed. She said, "Initially the thought of leaving made me feel as if I was cheating. I was so nervous that it was hard for me to look at my boss. I was sure he could see that I'm not really happy and might leave." Yet she vacillated between feeling guilty about thoughts of leaving and feeling excited about being desirable to other companies.

Eventually, she became consumed with the fantasy of leaving. Marian chuckled, "I'd catch myself sometimes daydreaming about life with another company. Once I saw myself joining this new company, and they gave me roses the first day! I had an office full of cards with greetings and best wishes from my new colleagues. They really wanted me. I got this large salary increase, my own secretary, and a supervisor willing to be my sponsor." Reflectively she said, "I wondered if it's really any better in the long run to leave. I now know what it was like for my friend Angela when she got tired of being the good girl and being taken for granted. She was miserable. I'm sorry I didn't understand her pain better then. Now I'm in her shoes. I see how it can happen when you're feeling dissatisfied and an enticing offer comes along." Stoically, Marian asks, "I wonder if my company would make me a counteroffer if I told them I was leaving?" She paused for a second and said, "You know what gets me about that question? I don't know if they would!"

Marian had begun the process of *distancing*. She was beginning to experience the symptoms in the following box.

Reactions: Distancing

✓ Fantasize about leaving
✓ Have disassociated feelings with her work/organization
✓ Respond to recruiters and headhunters
✓ Wonder if her organization would make a counteroffer

Visualizing yourself in another environment can be a release valve. Flirtation results from a need to be recognized and feel valued from the work relationship to which you're commit-

Figure 3-1. Emotional reactions to a troubled work relationship.

Emotional Reaction	Your Reaction
Distancing	• Lowered involvement with work • Fantasies about leaving the organization • Responded to headhunters • Disassociation from company events, employees, positions • Active testing of your value on the open market
Disengaging	• Lack of interest in the company and work relationship • Lack of commitment to project or employees • Boredom • Political disengagement from company politics • Loss of passion for work, company
Confronting	• Anger • Active disagreement; provocateur • Inappropriate response to provocation • Verbal/physical confrontation • Strong physical/emotional responses (physical illness, depression, paranoia) • Cry for help/attention/resolution • Avoidance by others
Acknowledging	• Recognition of problem in work relationship • Acceptance of problem • Initial reactions of shock, hurt, betrayal, fear • Fear/concern of how individual or organization will look to others • Recognition of individual/organization's role in the problem • Obvious physical response
Fix It—Make It Right	• Promises, promises • Earnest work to resolve issues • Motions to resolve issues • Previously withheld perks—raises, promotions, new assignments—secured • Commitment to improve • Wait-and-see attitude, until first mistake • Attempts to rekindle lost feeling • Lots of attention, special treatment
Ending It	• Resurfacing of same problems • Irreconcilable differences • Recognition of different needs from organization • Lack of confidence on longevity of change • Compromised trust • Emotionally moved on • Had enough, can't take anymore • Lack of caring

- Your exclusion from meetings
- Avoidance of contact with you
- Your phone calls unreturned
- Delay in responding to your requests repeatedly
- Documentation of your behavior
- Less feedback to you

- Lack of interest in what you're doing
- Lack of verbal, written, or visible support for you
- Little or no direction, supervision; ignores you/your needs
- Your name or other personal information forgotten

- Creation of stress to keep you off balance
- Condescending tone used to speak to you
- Inappropriate language with you
- Quick temper
- Unrealistic deadlines, expectations for you
- Strong nonverbal signals to you
- Put-downs in meeting or publicly
- Avoidance of contact with you
- Reassignment with distance from you
- Special assignment with no teeth

- Formal recognition of problem (performance review, warning of poor performance, threat)
- Informal feedback on relationship issues
- Attempts to identify the problem
- Eliciting your perspective on issues
- Intervention of others to help/face resolution
- Concern expressed regarding implication/impact on person, supervisor, organization
- Formal commitment/contract to work issues

- Requests for you to "hang in there"
- Actual commitments to work issue
- Your requests met
- Perks provided
- Meetings with key hierarchy to understand problem
- Clear performance expectations with timelines
- Reprimands to appropriate people
- Promises

- Resurfacing of same problems
- Request for resignation
- Termination
- Lack of trust displayed
- Lack of confidence in your judgment
- Totally disinterested
- No commitment to continue working issue
- Decision to let relationship go

ted. It makes you feel good and, often, important. To have recruiters tell you that you're wanted and to act upon that desire
can be seductive. This situation is like being in a relationship
with someone for several years who you feel takes you for
granted; then someone new comes along who gives you some
attention, is understanding, is appreciative, and values you, and
you consider ending your long-term relationship. Yet, you can't
just walk away. In work relationships too, the emotional bond
can be just as difficult to break as in a personal relationship.

Boredom: Is This All There Is?

Cynthia, a middle-level manager, was reflecting on the moment when she realized her work relationship was in serious
trouble:

> I got so bored that I just couldn't concentrate. I felt pi-
> geonholed. I had asked for more responsibility. I
> wanted the organization to invest in me, give me bet-
> ter assignments, more exposure. It didn't. I just kept
> getting the same old work, and I got sick of it. Then I
> started procrastinating. I would find other activities
> outside work that I found more challenging and I
> poured all my energies into those outside projects. By
> the time I got to work, I didn't have any interest or en-
> ergy left, and I was glad. I felt as if I had moved be-
> yond the relationship. But I couldn't quit. At first, I
> kept thinking this was only temporary. Eventually, it
> caught up with me. I received a horrible performance
> appraisal, and my boss said I had six months to shape
> up. I started wondering why should I shape up only
> to continue with this boring relationship. I guess
> that's when I started to self-destruct.

Cynthia was pouring all of her creative energies into activities outside her job to offset what appeared to be boredom. In
reality, Cynthia felt stagnated, unchallenged, and unsponsored
at work. She was creating a totally separate avenue for her talents and sources of positive recognition. In terms of our model,

Cynthia had become almost totally *disengaged* from her organization.

Reactions: Disengagement

✓ Lost interest in her assignments and her company
✓ Lacked commitment to any project and people
✓ Was bored
✓ Had disengaged politically
✓ Lost her passion for work

Boredom is a warning sign of something amiss in the relationship. It suggests that the working relationship is no longer stimulating. Perhaps the relationship is stagnated. The thought that this boredom may be a permanent condition is frightening. Typically in this situation we focus more on activities and people outside work, which give us recognition and value. In fact, at key periods in life—especially when you're approaching the age milestones of 30, 35, 40, 50—you begin to wonder how your job makes a difference. You begin to ask yourself, "What do I want my life to stand for? When I die what do I want to be known for? What'll be on my tombstone?"

Boredom is a response to feelings that you can't grow in your work relationship anymore; your job has reached its peak, and you have reached a plateau. You are no longer motivated because you feel as if you're not growing and learning. When this happens, you will find yourself daydreaming, being late to meetings, not focused on the task, missing deadlines, and eventually not performing against your expectations. Eventually your performance is affected, and your relationship suffers even more.

Everything's a Fight: I'm Mad

Sue had gotten to the point that she regularly took three aspirin before she got out of her car to go into the office. She asked nervously, "Do you think I'm addicted?" She told us that as she drove to work, she would rehearse how she would let loose on everyone at work and set them straight: "Here I was at the red light. I was just practicing arguing with myself. I was shaking my head, throwing my hands around, twisting my face. I was into how I would do it at work. I looked over to the next car, and there was this man who looked shocked. I sneered at him. Then I put my foot on the pedal and sped off." Suddenly she stopped laughing and said, "Maybe I am losing it. I think this relationship is making me crazy." She confessed that every day she was so riled by the time she got to work that she felt prepared to take on anyone. She resolved that if anyone made a joke about her, looked at her funny, or excluded her from a meeting again, she would give them a mouthful. She was tired of constructive feedback. "How dare they try to mess with me!" she'd find herself saying in the mirror. "I'm not going to take this anymore. In fact, I'll get a jump on them before they try to pounce on me!" Every day, she left work as she started, taking three aspirins.

Sue was in the *confrontation* stage. She not only responded to provocation; she was a provocateur. She created crisis and was easily manipulated by others. She knew her behavior was seen as inappropriate and unprofessional, but at some point she had stopped caring. Sue's symptoms clearly belong to this stage.

Reactions: Confrontation

✓ Provoking disagreements and uncontrolled response
✓ Eliciting a strong negative organizational reaction
✓ Having a strong physical or emotional reaction (physical illness, depression, uncontrolled anger)
✓ Engaging in verbal/physical confrontation

Although Sue's situation may appear extreme, it is not unusual. Repeated disagreements, disputes, and negative posturing are key indications that a work relationship is in trouble. They suggest that you and your employer or colleagues have gotten into the animosity rut, which occurs when you or others question each other's integrity and truthfulness and you feel that you're the only one who will stand up for yourself. You feel as if you have no mentor or sponsor, and you're on the defensive. You refuse to lose one more bit of pride and self-esteem, so you fight to preserve yourself and your dignity. However, unknowingly you're digging a deeper hole because in the process, what you fear the most is occurring:

- Your colleagues avoid you
- People tell you what they think you want to hear to avoid confrontation
- You start getting assignments that require you to work more by yourself
- You stop receiving constructive feedback

You begin to realize this is a vicious cycle, but you just can't seem to get off the merry-go-round. So you fight harder, and still you're sinking deeper.

Sick All the Time

Erica sighed, "I've been to the doctor almost every month for the last year. I feel as if my body is falling apart. At first I thought I was a hypochondriac, but my doctor's test results confirmed I was really sick. Then I got scared. I can't remember a time in my life when I've been so repeatedly sick. My doctor asked me to keep a diary of key events, stressful situations, periods of frustration and anger, periods of happiness and peace. I realized she thought I was a little out of control." The results were an eye opener for Erica because she saw a consistent pattern: "I was so surprised. Whenever I had a major project review with my supervisor or team members, I got sick immediately afterward. My absentee rate was 100 percent higher than last year." She then acknowledged, "It is hard for me to admit that I am feeling miserable about my work relationship. I'd never had any relationship that was a problem. This makes me feel as if I'm a failure. I assumed I was the problem, that things were my fault." Erica also realized that she had few entries of happiness and peace in her journal: "I can't remember the last time I was just silly and laughed. I spend almost no time with my friends and close relatives. I have no interest outside work. When I have a free moment, I usually spend it in bed, alone." Although she was relieved with this revelation, she was frightened about what it meant and ruminated, "Does this mean I'm going wacko?"

Erica had reached the *acknowledging* stage that her work relationship was in serious trouble. Her body had given her signals, but she had not connected the stress of her work relationship with her illnesses. Rather, she had become adept at repressing her feelings and turning her fear inward. The situation became too much for her body to handle. The illnesses were cries for help. Her reactions are common to this stage.

Reactions: Acknowledgment of Problem
✓ Recognition of a problem in the relationship
✓ Feelings of shock, hurt, betrayal, fear
✓ Physical reaction

Our bodies are wonderful message centers that can convey to us through physical pain, emotional distress, or both what we don't want to hear and show us what we don't want to see. Some of the symptoms are headaches, back pain, earaches, gastrointestinal problems, female reproductive problems, rashes, eye twitches, and frequent colds. An increase in illness linked to stress in a work relationship is a major warning sign. The task is to listen to our bodies and understand what they're communicating to us.

Work Is No Fun Anymore

Wanda, a thirty-year-old chemical engineer and research scientist, was having a very difficult time relating to her immediate supervisor and felt that the company's strategy was adversely affecting the quality of its research and development. Even so, she was involved in a research project that could significantly improve the quality of life for children born with a certain genetic defect:

> This project kept me motivated and driving for its successful completion. I wanted to do something that mattered. So I chose to ignore all the problems such as lack of support, no feedback, mixed messages. These problems were distracting, and I felt powerless to change them anyway. I put them in the back of my mind—the hurt feelings and lack of trust I had for my spineless supervisor and the company. Then came the final insult: I was told to accelerate the project because my budget had been cut by four months. I was furious and felt cheated and unsupported. My supervisor knew I was angry, but he chose to ignore it until I completed the project. I knew he was using me for his own agenda. Still, I was compulsive about this project so I pushed it through successfully anyway.
>
> Afterwards I was given a half-step promotion, an out-of-sequence raise, a lot of recognition by my senior management, and the next top assignment. I thought I'd be jubilant, but I wasn't. I felt so empty, so burned out. You know, I still feel indifferent. As hard as I try, I can't get started. I simply don't care about this work anymore. In fact, I've vowed never to care so much about anything related to this job. I cannot disguise my indifferent feelings for the company. I don't care how the company views me or my work. I feel their attempts to make everything okay are too little, too late.

Reactions: Fix It—Make It Right
✓ Recent raise and promotion
✓ Change in assignment
✓ Hope of a positive outcome

(text continued on p. 64)

Figure 3-2. Emotional reaction indicator.

Directions: Select the number on the scale that corresponds to the intensity of this emotional reaction for you—for example, 1 if it feels negligibly intense or 5

1 Negligibly Intense Emotional Reaction	2 Your Reaction	Mildly Intense	3 Moderately Inten My Intensity Dimension
Distancing	• Lowered involvement with work • Fantasies about leaving the organization • Responded to headhunters • Disassociation from company events, employees, positions • Active testing of your value on the open market		
Disengaging	• Lack of interest in the company and work relationship • Lack of commitment to project or employees • Boredom • Political disengagement from company politics • Loss of passion for work, company		
Confronting	• Anger • Active disagreement; provocateur • Inappropriate response to provocation • Verbal/physical confrontation • Strong physical/emotional responses (physical illness, depression, paranoia) • Cry for help/attention/resolution • Avoidance by others		
Acknowledging	• Recognition of problem in work relationship • Acceptance of problem • Initial reactions of shock, hurt, betrayal, fear • Fear/concern of how individual or organization will look to others • Recognition of individual/organization's role in the problem • Obvious physical response		
Fix It—Make It Right	• Promises, promises • Earnest work to resolve issues • Motions to resolve issues • Previously withheld perks—raises, promotions, new assignments—secured • Commitment to improve • Wait-and-see attitude, until first mistake • Attempts to rekindle lost feeling • Lots of attention, special treatment		
Ending It	• Resurfacing of same problems • Irreconcilable differences • Recognition of different needs from organization • Lack of confidence on longevity of change • Compromised trust • Emotionally moved on • Had enough, can't take anymore • Lack of caring		

if it feels extremely intense. Place that number in the "My Intensity Reaction" box. Then select the number that reflects how your organization is responding to trouble in your relationship, and place that number in the "Its Intensity Dimension" box.

4 Very Intense Organization's Reaction	5 Extremely Intense Its Intensity Dimension
• Your exclusion from meetings • Avoidance of contact with you • Your phone calls unreturned • Delay in responding to your requests repeatedly • Documentation of your behavior • Falling feedback to you	
• Lack of interest in what you're doing • Lack of verbal, written, or visible support for you • Little or no direction, supervision; ignores you/your needs • Your name or other personal information forgotten	
• Creation of stress to keep you off balance • Condescending tone used to speak to you • Inappropriate language with you • Quick temper • Unrealistic deadlines, expectations for you • Strong nonverbal signals to you • Put-downs in meeting or publicly • Avoidance of contact with you • Reassignment with distance from you • Special assignment with no teeth	
• Formal recognition of problem (performance review, warning of poor performance, threat) • Informal feedback on relationship issues • Attempts to identify the problem • Eliciting your perspective on issues • Intervention of others to help/face resolution • Concern expressed regarding implication/impact on person, supervisor, organization • Formal commitment/contract to work issues	
• Requests for you to "hang in there" • Actual commitments to work issue • Your requests met • Perks provided • Meetings with key hierarchy to understand problem • Clear performance expectations with timelines • Reprimands to appropriate people • Promises	
• Resurfacing of same problems • Request for resignation • Termination • Lack of trust displayed • Lack of confidence in your judgment • Totally disinterested • No commitment to continue working issue • Decision to let relationship go	

Wanda's situation points to the ineffective impact of "desperation" perks when a woman's trust is severely compromised and she has become totally disengaged. Wanda shows symptoms of being in the fix it—make it right stage.

Conclusion

You may notice that none of the stories reflected the last uncoupling stage, "Ending It." We purposely did not indicate which of these relationships ended because we wanted to focus your attention on how these women experienced trouble in paradise. We want you to explore the messages you've received from yourself and others as you experience difficulties in your work relationships.

As the case studies illustrated, regardless of who precipitated the relationship difficulty or why, the trouble affects both you and the organization. To help you identify the intensity of both your and your organization's reaction to the trouble in your relationship, use the worksheet displayed in Figure 3-2 and the scoring grid in Figure 3-3.

Where Do I Go From Here?

As we stated at the beginning of Part II, this chapter was designed to heighten your awareness of any potential trouble in your paradise. It would not be unusual if you feel ready to do something to fix it right now. As a career and professional woman, you're trained to solve problems, and you're darned good at it. Surely you can get your relationship back on track or resolved in one way or another.

Our advice, however, is to do nothing right now. Sit with what you're experiencing. Go inside your head, your heart, and your stomach, and tap your innermost thoughts about what you've learned about your work relationship. You're now equipped with some of the knowledge to resolve your work relationship issue or create an entirely new one, but you don't have it all. Partial knowledge can be dangerous because it gives the illusion that you have all you need to know to move ahead. Chapter 4 provides another piece of the puzzle. It will take you one step closer to understanding the full impact of your work relationship.

Figure 3-3. Scoring and interpretive grid for the emotional reaction indicator.

Scoring: You will have two scores, yours and the organization's. Add the scores under "My Intensity Dimension," write them here _____. Add the scores under "Its Intensity Dimension," write them here _____. Identify the interpretation level that reflects your scores and

Emotional Reaction	Your Reaction	Organization's Reaction
Level 1 1–10	Your emotional reactions are under control or are very repressed. Scores over 5 suggest that your intensity is appropriate for a relationship experiencing minimal difficulty. Scores 5 and below suggest that you're either out of touch with your emotions by successfully regressing them (i.e., putting them in the back of your mind) or that you've gotten past the emotional roller coaster and are clearly in the healing or healed phase. As a check, see if the behaviors you describe match your intensity indicator. If they do then great. It supports your self-assessment. If your behaviors are different, (i.e., more intense), you need to step back and identify where there is a disconnect between what you rated and what you do.	Your organization's emotional reaction suggests that it's having a mild emotional reaction to your relationship. Scores 5 and below suggest that the organization is experiencing almost no adverse emotional reaction to your work relationship. Scores approaching 10 (8–10) are indicative of some increased emotional reactions.
Level 2 11–20	This is an emotionally trying period for you. You may find that the intensity of your feelings vacillate across the six emotional reactions. Scores near 16 suggest that you're approaching or are on the borderline for emotional reactions that could be totally consuming. This is a serious signal.	The organization is having increased negative emotional reactions to its relationship with you. Something is amiss in its view of your work relationship. This is a period to get clear and work issues. If issues aren't resolved, then the intensity of their emotional reactions to you will increase. This is the period when group think emerges.
Level 3 21–30	You're on the emotional roller coaster. Your reactions to this troubled work relationship are intense enough for you to take a time-out. In this time-out you should reflect on those behaviors you've identified and create a plan to reduce your intensity level in at least two reactions. This is serious. If you can't reduce your intensity indicator, seek professional help.	The organization is on an emotional roller coaster in response to its relationship with you. This spells trouble. In most cases, the organization is deciding if you should be dismissed or transferred. You need to get to the bottom of the issue immediately.

Comparison of Your and the Organization's Emotional Reaction

It will be very helpful if you compare the level of your and the organization's emotional reaction. Indicate the level of your reaction _____ and the organization's level _____. Are these levels the same, slightly different, or markedly different? What does this tell you?

4
Problems Are Messages

Several years ago one of my friends called me in a panic. She had been interviewing women who had been in top executive positions for seven to ten years. She said it was as if they got suited up, got on the bus, and went to the games, but . . . they never got off the bench. At first they were hopeful, but after a few years they had become resigned to the reality that they would never quite belong. She said that she found more alcoholism, clinical depression, and anorexia-bulimia in this group of women than she had even seen.

Anne Wilson Schaef, *Women's Reality*

These women obviously had earned the right for rewarding, high-profile executive positions with their companies; it was natural for them to expect the ring and all the benefits of marriage. What went wrong? Clearly the issue wasn't their performance or unrealistic expectations. We can safely assume that they had overcome the myriad of obstacles that typically confront most professional women. For example, they had to be smarter, work harder, swallow their pride, and bite their bottom lip to hold in what they really wanted to say. They may have watched their male peers surpass them repeatedly. There was an expectation that they would appear less feminine and should fit in with the men. They smiled when they didn't want to. They went beyond the call of duty to prove that they could be top performers *and*, for some, good mothers. With all of these challenges, these women were expected to be team players, love what they were doing, and be totally committed to their work relationships.

The answer to the question, "What went wrong?" lies not in these women's performance and commitment to their work but in differing views of their work relationship. The women wanted marriage; their organizations didn't. The reality is that countless numbers of women who prepared themselves to fight the good fight and win their rightful place in the boardroom of America's corporations have found that they couldn't break the glass ceiling—or, if they made it, their accomplishments were negated by the belief that they're fulfilling an "affirmative action quota" or they "slept their way to the top."

Schaef's opening quotation presents a disturbingly accurate picture of what happens to women when there is a great difference between what they want, dream, hope, and deserve as compared with reality. Our experience has shown that the greater the different there is between what we want and what we have, the more intense are our reactions. These reactions, known as *cognitive dissonance*, are played out in feelings of anger, rage, resentment, depression, frustration, illness, apathy, and fear.[1]

We all carry pictures in our heads about who we think we should or could be. These visual images represent our hopes and our dreams, as well as those things that we believe we deserve. We are motivated by our pictures, and we strive to make them a reality. When our reality isn't the same as our pictures, we experience cognitive dissonance. This dissonance can show up anywhere along a continuum from subtle stress to manic depression (Figure 4-1). The result can be serious health problems—heart attack, strokes, cancer, diabetes, ulcers—all of which have increased significantly for women over the past twenty years.

Often we are not aware we are in danger until our symptoms are very pronounced. We are so wrapped up in our com-

Figure 4-1. Cognitive dissonance.

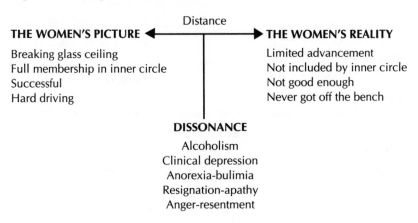

	Distance	
THE WOMEN'S PICTURE ◄──────────►		THE WOMEN'S REALITY
Breaking glass ceiling		Limited advancement
Full membership in inner circle		Not included by inner circle
Successful		Not good enough
Hard driving		Never got off the bench

DISSONANCE
Alcoholism
Clinical depression
Anorexia-bulimia
Resignation-apathy
Anger-resentment

mitments to our work, to the investments and sacrifices we have made on our road to so-called career success, that we don't even realize how other areas of our lives have been affected. We're on autopilot, hoping that we'll find the rewards we seek and that somehow it will all balance out.

Balancing the Personal, Work, and Social Spheres

Most of us struggle to balance three major areas in our lives: personal, social, and work. We have been raised to believe that we can have it all because we have opportunities that our mothers lacked. We are better educated, financially independent, career oriented, and sexually freer. The truth is that we *can* have it all, but we need balance.

Most of our mothers' personal, social, and professional lives centered around one area, the home. This made their roles clearer, more predictable, and generally easier to manage than our own. But a lot has changed in the past thirty years, and it will change even more by the year 2000 when, it is anticipated, four of every five women will work outside the home, thereby making the interplay of work, personal, and social responsibilities that much harder to coordinate.[2]

Working women today have three separate spheres to manage, each with a separate set of rules, expectations, and relationships. Rather than being the silent background partners in our husband's or partner's quest to pursue their careers, we say, "My turn," and profess that we can do it all. We juggle by taking from one area of our lives and giving to another, a balancing act that has left many women exhausted and dissatisfied. If you are to believe TV ads and the magazine covers, we should all look like Whitney Houston or Cindy Crawford, work like Hillary Rodham Clinton, cook like Julia Child, raise children like Donna Reed, and make love like Mata Hari—all in a day. Whew! No wonder we're stressed out.

We designed the Message Quiz, shown as Figure 4-2, to give you a perspective on what stressors you're reacting to. We can't guarantee that you won't have any stress by the end of this chapter, but you will know what's causing your stress and why. Once you understand the dynamics of your situation, you'll be motivated to start making healthy choices.

Take the Message Quiz now to measure three general factors:

1. *Balance factor:* How these messages affect your life.
2. *Concern factor:* Your level of concern with these messages.
3. *Frequency factor:* How often you have received these messages.

These measures are captured in two scoring and interpretation charts: Figure 4-3 for the Balance factor and Figure 4-4 for the Concern and Frequency factors. The higher the scores are, the more danger you're in.

Scoring and Charting

Balance factor: Add all the True answers for questions 1–25 and multiply that number by 3. Place an X in the number range corresponding to your score in the "Personal" column in Figure 4-3. Repeat these instructions for the Social (questions 26–50) and Work (questions 51–75) spheres as well.

Figure 4-2. The Message Quiz.

Mark the following statements as True or Not True. Then indicate whether you are concerned about the message by circling *yes* or *no*. (In the "Messages" column, INT="I've noticed that . . ." and PTM="People tell me that . . ."

True	Not True	Concerned	*Messages*
☐	☐	Y or N	1. INT I've gained or lost weight without meaning to.
☐	☐	Y or N	2. INT I'm not sleeping well.
☐	☐	Y or N	3. INT I hurt in more places (e.g., back, neck, stomach) than I used to.
☐	☐	Y or N	4. INT sex feels more like work than fun.
☐	☐	Y or N	5. INT I don't feel sexy anymore.
☐	☐	Y or N	6. INT I've been to a doctor more this year than ever before.
☐	☐	Y or N	7. INT I eat junk food all the time.
☐	☐	Y or N	8. INT I'm too tired to cook dinner.
☐	☐	Y or N	9. INT I haven't taken a bubble bath in a long time.
☐	☐	Y or N	10. INT I care less about how I look.
☐	☐	Y or N	11. INT I drink alcohol often.
☐	☐	Y or N	12. INT I keep wanting to change my look.
☐	☐	Y or N	13. INT my house is always a mess.
☐	☐	Y or N	14. INT it's harder for me to get up in the morning.
☐	☐	Y or N	15. INT although I sleep, I never feel rested.
☐	☐	Y or N	16. INT I never listen to music anymore.
☐	☐	Y or N	17. PTM I look tired all the time.
☐	☐	Y or N	18. INT I can't stand any type of criticism.
☐	☐	Y or N	19. PTM I've never looked better.
☐	☐	Y or N	20. INT it's getting harder and harder for me to concentrate.
☐	☐	Y or N	21. INT being a superwoman is important to me.
☐	☐	Y or N	22. INT I work hard to prove that I can handle it all.
☐	☐	Y or N	23. INT I don't laugh as much as I used to.
☐	☐	Y or N	24. PTM I'm too sensitive; I take everything personally.
☐	☐	Y or N	25. PTM I act as if I'm always tense or moody.
☐	☐	Y or N	26. PTM that I'm no fun to be around anymore.
☐	☐	Y or N	27. INT I support my friends more than they support me.
☐	☐	Y or N	28. INT I never have enough time to spend with friends.
☐	☐	Y or N	29. INT I'm daydreaming more about having fun in my life.
☐	☐	Y or N	30. INT I only read business-related magazines and books; I don't read for fun anymore.
☐	☐	Y or N	31. INT all my friends are from work.
☐	☐	Y or N	32. INT at parties, all I talk about is work.
☐	☐	Y or N	33. INT I don't have a social life.
☐	☐	Y or N	34. INT none of my friends are from my job.
☐	☐	Y or N	35. INT I'm more comfortable dating someone from work.
☐	☐	Y or N	36. INT I'm putting more time in social and community projects in the evenings and on weekends.

True	Not True	Concerned	Messages
☐	☐	Y or N	37. INT I feel better about my volunteer work than my job.
☐	☐	Y or N	38. INT I have not taken time out for my family.
☐	☐	Y or N	39. INT I'm feeling more lonely, as if no one cares for me.
☐	☐	Y or N	40. INT work is not enough for me; I need more outlets.
☐	☐	Y or N	41. INT I don't know what to do with my free time.
☐	☐	Y or N	42. PTM I don't take enough time off to smell the roses.
☐	☐	Y or N	43. INT I am fantasizing more about my relationship with my significant other.
☐	☐	Y or N	44. INT I want a more spiritual component in my life.
☐	☐	Y or N	45. INT I'm thinking more about getting married.
☐	☐	Y or N	46. INT I'm thinking more about getting a divorce or breaking up a relationship.
☐	☐	Y or N	47. INT I'm thinking more about having children.
☐	☐	Y or N	48. INT I'm ready to commit to a personal relationship with someone.
☐	☐	Y or N	49. INT getting balance in my life makes me feel and function better.
☐	☐	Y or N	50. INT I avoid getting too close to my colleagues.
☐	☐	Y or N	51. PTM that some things happen at work you just have to live with.
☐	☐	Y or N	52. PTM at work I'm not like the rest of them; I'm the exception.
☐	☐	Y or N	53. PTM that it's not clear what I'm trying to prove at work.
☐	☐	Y or N	54. PTM that I don't let negative stereotypes about women stop me on the job.
☐	☐	Y or N	55. INT at work everybody else seems to know things before I do.
☐	☐	Y or N	56. INT men at work stop talking when I enter the room.
☐	☐	Y or N	57. PTM at work that I have a chip on my shoulder.
☐	☐	Y or N	58. PTM at work that I don't play by the rules.
☐	☐	Y or N	59. PTM at work that I'm not a team player.
☐	☐	Y or N	60. PTM at work that I don't want to pay my dues.
☐	☐	Y or N	61. PTM I don't smile anymore at work.
☐	☐	Y or N	62. INT I have the worst headaches right before I meet with my boss.
☐	☐	Y or N	63. INT at work I can't sit through an entire meeting without getting anxious or agitated.
☐	☐	Y or N	64. PTM that I need to choose my battles more carefully at work.
☐	☐	Y or N	65. INT men around me are getting promoted and I'm not.
☐	☐	Y or N	66. PTM that I act more cautious around women peers at work.
☐	☐	Y or N	67. INT I care less about helping younger women in my business.
☐	☐	Y or N	68. INT at work I'm constantly getting angry with men.
☐	☐	Y or N	69. PTM that at work that I'm the "golden child."
☐	☐	Y or N	70. PTM that they envy the fact that I run my own show.
☐	☐	Y or N	71. PTM that I have "attitude" at work.
☐	☐	Y or N	72. PTM I can't change the way things are—business is business.
☐	☐	Y or N	73. INT I have a nagging sense that things aren't okay at work, but I don't know what's wrong.
☐	☐	Y or N	74. PTM at work that I need to be more trusting of others.
☐	☐	Y or N	75. PTM that I have persevered in this business despite the odds.

Figure 4-3. Scoring and interpretation for the Message Quiz: the balance factor.

Scoring Range	Signal Light	<<——SPHERES——>> Personal	Social	Work	Interpretation By Signal Light	By Fluctuation in Ranges
61–75	Red Light ● ○ ○				Danger! Stop immediately. There are a lot of concerned messages from other people and yourself. Deal with them immediately. It's serious. *Action:* Make a plan. Get outside help from a counselor or trusted friend. Commit to a date.	Danger! Stop immediately. A score for any sphere falling in this range spells trouble. It means that you've received a lot of concerned messages about this sphere(s) of your life and that you're out of balance. In fact, if all three of your spheres fall in this range, then you're consistently out of balance in each major aspect of your life. *Action:* Reassess what the message is telling you; then set priorities that force you to choose what you want to do in each sphere. If you score high in two spheres, you're predominantly out of balance. Again, reassess what the messages are telling you. Usually the sphere with the lowest score is how you're coping with your imbalance. Try to set priorities for your two remaining high-scoring spheres. These priorities should help you focus on what you will or won't do. If it's high in just one sphere, you may want to consider what you need to do to get more in balance.
46–60	Flashing Red Light ☀				Pause. Impending danger. The frequency of messages suggests a need for serious reflection. Get focused on what the signals are telling you. *Action:* Talk with a trusted friend, a work associate, or a counselor. Ask for feedback. Listen; don't defend. Develop a plan of action.	Pause! Right now! A score for any of these spheres is a signal of impending danger. You're perilously close to crossing the danger zone (red light). *Action:* Consider which and how many of your scores fall in the flashing red light zone. If all three are the same, it's time to take serious stock. Create more balance by eliminating one thing from each sphere. Don't substitute it with a new positive thing. If you find variability in your score—for example, the personal is 54, but the social is 25 and the work is 63—then you're completely out of balance, and should try to reduce your intensity in the high scoring spheres.
31–45	Yellow Light ○ ● ○				Slow down. Proceed with caution. The increased messages are clear warnings that something's amiss. *Action:* Reflect on why you are receiving messages. Make a commitment to resolve specific issues now. Take time out and plan.	Slow down! Caution! A score in any sphere is a warning sign that things aren't all right in that sphere(s). *Action:* Take stock of the messages you're receiving and what they are suggesting. Again, note if and when there may be variability in the score for each range. Ask yourself what it means for you.

16-30	Green Light 	All's clear. There is a minimum number of concerned messages. Your awareness level and responses are appropriate. Caution: Don't be lulled into belief of permanent security. *Action:* Do a bimonthly message check. Ask for feedback.	Go! All clear. Messages in any of these three spheres mean you're basically balanced in that sphere(s). You're appropriating the right amount of focus to that sphere(s). You know what it takes and means to be balanced. Congratulations. *Action:* Watch out! Check for variability. If your score is green, for example, in work, you may be compensating for work pressures through an aggressive social agenda. Or if personal is high (red light) and work and social are green, you could be ignoring those concerned personal messages by ensuring more balance in the social and work spheres.
1-15	U-Turn 	One of two situations is occurring: (1) Things are going exceptionally well. There is an absence of negative signals, and this matches your perceptions. OR (2) You're out of touch with what really is going on in your life. You're not hearing or allowing yourself to experience the signals. *Action:* In either case, reexamine your messages. Have a trusted colleague or friend take the quiz by "being you." Compare your responses with his or hers.	U-Turn. Check It Out! Either you're one of those persons who achieved what most of the world wants—absence of stress in each sphere(s) or you're doing a good job of fooling yourself or ignoring other people's concerned messages. *Action:* Retake the Message Quiz. Then have someone who knows you well take the quiz as if he or she were you. Compare the two sets of scores.

Scoring Notes:

It's *smooth sailing* when you have consistently low scores across all three spheres. This is a very positive indicator that you have appropriated your time and energies to each of the three spheres of your life.

You're out of wack when you have consistently high scores across all three spheres. This is trouble. It suggests that you have not appropriated time, energy, and resources for any of the three spheres. You could be feeling stressed out, overwhelmed, and out of control.

It'll be a bumpy ride when you don't have a consistent pattern. Your scores are scattered all over the chart. You need to investigate why your spheres are out of balance. Are you putting attention on one sphere and ignoring others?

Figure 4-4. Scoring and interpretation for the Message Quiz: the frequency and concern level factors.

Scoring Range	Signal Light	Message of Frequency	My Level of Concern	INTERPRETATION By Signal Light
61–75	Red Light (●○○)			Danger! Stop immediately. If both your messages and concern level are high, you're functioning in reality. You recognize that this has to be addressed immediately. You must commit to action. This is serious.
46–60	Flashing Red Light			Pause. Impending danger. The frequency of messages suggests a need for serious reflection. Get focused on what signals are telling you. If both scores are similar, you're getting consistent messages of impending danger, and you're hearing them. Now is the time to take action before you encounter more difficulties. If you don't, it will get more problematic.
31–45	Yellow Light (○●○)			Slow down. Proceed with caution. You are getting increased messages that are clear warnings. Something's amiss. If both scores are in the same range, you're hearing cautionary messages. Make sure you've slowed down enough to determine if you've missed any messages.
16–30	Green Light (○○●)			All's clear. There is a minimum number of concerned messages. Your awareness level and responses are appropriate. If both scores are similar, you're getting few concern message and your level of concern is appropriate because you're not generating undue anxiety. Remember, if you don't stay attuned to your messages, this light can change from green to yellow to red.
1–15	U-Turn			One of two situations is occurring at this period in your life: (1) Things are going exceptionally well. There is an absence of negative signals and your concern level is appropriate. This is a desirable state. OR (2) You're out of touch with what really is going on in your life. You're not hearing or allowing yourself to experience the signals or be concerned. You may have distanced yourself from reality and inappropriately negated all concern. In either case, reexamine your messages and concern level.

Scoring Notes: If your Message Frequency is high but your Level of Concern is one range lower, your concern is not quite as high as it should be. Conversely, if your Message Frequency is low and your Level of Concern is high, then you may be overly concerned. The greater the differences between these two ranges, the more attention you need to apply to decipher the lack of alignment.

Concern factor: Count the number of Yes (Y) answers. In the column "My Level of Concern" in Figure 4-4, place an X in the numeric range corresponding to your score.

Frequency factor: Count the number of True answers. Find the range that corresponds to your score in Figure 4-4, and place an X in the "Message Frequency" column.

The alignment of your Message Frequency and Concern Level serves as a reality check for you. The degree of alignment that you may or may not be experiencing is a function of how close these two are. The Message Quiz has three levels of alignment:

1. *Total alignment.* Your scores for Message Frequency (MF) and Concern Level (CL) fall in the same range—for example, your MF is 20 and CL is 25, so both are in the green light (16–30) range. This means that you have the appropriate concern level for the frequency of messages you've received. If you have total alignment with a red light, you need to turn that appropriate concern into action quickly.

2. *Slight misalignment.* There is one scoring range difference for MF and CL. This could mean that you're slightly more (or less) concerned than perhaps you should be, suggesting that a minor correction needs to be made in either your own awareness or your responses to the quiz, or you might need to review your answers to ensure that they truly reflect messages you've received or your true concern level.

3. *Total misalignment.* There is a two or more scoring range difference for MF and CL—for example, an MF of 70 and a CL of 45. This should be of significant concern to you, for it suggests that you're totally out of alignment. You may be receiving more concerned messages than you're taking seriously, or you may be totally oblivious to these problem messages. To delve deeper into the exact problem, try this:

a. Have someone who knows you well take this quiz based on how he or she has experienced you.

b. Retake this quiz, and compare the responses to your

first quiz. Did your score come out pretty much the same? Were there differences? If so, in what areas are they?

c. Compare your two quiz scores to those of the person who is helping you. Are they similar or different?

d. If your scores still suggest total misalignment, it's time to go to a professional counselor to help you sort out why.

Comparing the Pictures and the Reality

Many of the women we interviewed had been stuck in work relationship dilemmas for years. It's not that they weren't smart; they simply didn't know how to go about getting unstuck. Don't let this happen to you! Stop ruminating and start focusing on understanding your situation and creating different pictures, realities, and reactions.

Take all that you've learned in Chapters 1–4 and apply it to your own personal case study of your work relationship. Taking the time to do this now will save you hours of frustrating self-examination in the future. The best technique we know for helping you come to grips with a troubled work relationship is to capture your pictures, realities, and corresponding emotional reactions on paper. Recall that this was the technique used in Figure 4-1 earlier in this chapter.

Begin by answering questions for: (1) pictures, then (2) realities, and finally, (3) dissonance/emotional reactions. Complete your case study by filling in the boxes in Figure 4-5.

Now that you can graphically assess your work relationship, decide where you stand on the following issues:

1. Am I experiencing enough stress or dissonance to take some action?

    [ ] Yes
    [ ] No

2. I know that at this point I have two choices: (1) change my pictures or (2) change my reality. Which option is more appealing to me?

Figure 4-5. Assessing your work relationship.

(1) PICTURES
What I want in a work relationship
What kind of relationship do I want to have with my organization or manager?
If I had this kind of relationship, what would I be feeling, thinking, and hearing from others?
What could I accomplish if I had this relationship?

(2) REALITIES
The current realities of my work relationship
What kind of relationship do I have with my organization or manager?
What messages am I receiving from the organization, others, and myself about this relationship?
What am I doing now with the relationship I have?

(3) DISSONANCE/EMOTIONAL REACTIONS

How well am I managing the dissonance and problem areas in my life?
How much distance is there between what I *want* (pictures) and what I *have* (realities)?
How is this distance affecting how I think, feel, and behave?

[ ]   Change my pictures
[ ]   Change my reality

3. What would I have to consider doing in order to make these changes?_____

_____

_____

4. How do I feel about that? What could sabotage my efforts?

_____

_____

_____

5. What power do I have? What can I control?_____

_____

_____

You are now ready for Part III. Because you know what's bothering you, we can help you work through these issues. Keep in mind that you are the only one who can choose what's right for you. In order to make decisions about what you want to do, you must first understand who you are. What are the values, principles, and beliefs that make you tick?

Part III

Choice: At the Crossroads

It is not easy to find happiness in ourselves, and it is not possible to find it elsewhere.

Agnes Repplier, in *Meditations for Women Who Do Too Much*

Do you want to live your life by constantly reacting to the circumstances that surround you? Or do you want to take responsibility and live according to the choices you make for yourself? You have just worked through a series of exercises in order to gain insight into your work relationship and the effect that it has on all parts of your life. Do you like where you are? Or is it time to change your work relationship? Psychologist Merle Shain put it best when she wrote: "There are really only two ways to approach life—as a victim or as a gallant fighter—and you must decide if you want to react, deal your own cards, or play with a stacked deck. And if you don't decide which way to play with life, it always plays with you."[1]

Part III is designed to help you deal your own cards and live your life by choice. The rewards of living "choicefully" are numerous:

- Your actions will be motivated by your own values, principles, and beliefs, not someone else's.

- You'll create your own happiness.
- You'll seek out and nurture healthy work relationships that support who you are and what you want to accomplish.
- You'll have an inner peace because you're choosing what's best for you.

The rewards won't come easily. You must be willing to take responsibility for your own actions and to embrace the changes that occur as a result of the choices you make.

Over the next two chapters, you will make decisions that will positively affect all aspects of your life. In Chapter 5, you will define and explore the values and beliefs that you hold dear. These personal fundamentals are the launching pad for the choices you will make. Chapter 6 discusses the concept of "doing choice" and walks you through the process. You'll learn why some women don't choose a new work relationship and instead choose misery, stuck in an unfulfilling work relationship.

You'll also be reacquainted with the women from Chapter 1 as we share the choices they made. Your own moment of truth comes at the end of Chapter 6 when you will be asked to make a choice to: stay in your work relationship and improve it, or leave it behind to pursue another work relationship that better meets your needs.

5

What Do You Really Want?

The important thing is this . . . to be willing at any moment to sacrifice what you are for what you could become.

Anonymous

Too much sanity may be madness, and the maddest of all is to see life as it is and not as it should be.

from *The Man of La Mancha*

With the fast pace of life, it isn't unusual to find yourself in a place you never intended to be, wondering what you have become. Just pausing to take a look at your life and your relationships, as you did in Chapter 4, can leave you feeling as if you need to make changes. You then begin to wonder, "What changes?" "When?" and "How will I know if it's right?" Much like the deer at night who is frozen by the headlights of a rapidly approaching car, you know that you have to make a move to save yourself but temporarily you're stuck.

There is a way to get unstuck, a way to figure out what you really want. The answer lies within you, and you must find the time necessary to reflect, understand what motivates you, and gather energy for action. One proven way to do this is through the power of visualization, an effective technique that athletes and performers regularly use to prepare themselves to do their best work. Shakti Gawain, author of *Creative Visualization*, describes it in this way:

> Creative visualization is the technique of using your imagination to create what you want in your life. There is nothing at all new, strange, or unusual about creative visualization. You are already using it every day, every minute in fact. . . . You use your imagination to create a clear image of something you wish to manifest. Then you continue to focus on the idea or picture regularly, giving it positive energy until it becomes objective reality . . . until you actually achieve what you have been visualizing.[1]

Visualization is a relaxing, self-empowering way to take a personal look at what could be rather than what is. How long has it been since you have thought about the possibilities of what you could become? The visualization exercises in this chapter will help you see your best self—the person you long to be. You will learn that you don't have to let what *is* control what *could be*. In short, you don't have to let what is true now remain true forever. Rather, you can find a way to have a work relationship that allows you to live your life in concert with your own closely held values and beliefs. This puts you in control of your own life choices so that you can act with integrity rather than in reaction to your situation or the actions of others.

Integrity is an important concept to consider as you think about making changes in your work relationships (and all other relationships in general). A strict definition of integrity is: "the quality or state of being complete or undivided; unimpaired; unmarred; an uncompromising adherence to a code of values; utter sincerity, honesty." Applying this definition to your own life, you have integrity when your life is integrated and complete. It feels wonderful when you make decisions and take actions that are consistent with what you truly believe. You find that others respect your decisions and understand your motives. Now that you are at a crossroads in your life where important decisions regarding your work and your life have to be made, it is critical that you get clear on your own values, beliefs, hopes, and dreams so that you can act with integrity.

The visualization exercises that follow are designed to help you get in touch with your own inner wishes and beliefs. Before we begin, we want to show you how these simple techniques can positively affect your life by sharing Elizabeth's story.

The Power of Visualization: Elizabeth's Experience

A year or so ago we were doing a workshop with a group of four very talented and unique women. They worked for an intelligence organization, and their work put them in almost constant physical danger. They had come to us to help them better understand how to get what they wanted and needed out of their work relationships. Like many other young women, they were struggling with the challenges of spreading their wings as women managers in a predominantly male organization. They considered themselves married to their organization; each could cite various sacrifices they had made for their work relationships. They impressed us as a serious bunch, dedicated to breaking the glass ceiling, and they wanted to talk organizational politics.

We were happy to oblige them, but first we felt it was important for each of them to get clear on what they wanted. After all, if you don't know where you're going, any road will get you there. Our friend, Kim Jones, had introduced us to this visualization technique, so we decided to give it a try.

One woman in particular, Elizabeth, had a dramatic response. After the visualization exercise, she looked at us with a shocked expression and said: "I don't believe what I saw!" The group gathered around her to hear about her experience, and, with a smile, this is what she said:

> In my vision I woke up in the morning, and I was so happy. I was pregnant! [She had just gone through a disappointing divorce and had no children.] I wasn't alone, but I couldn't tell who my husband was. I was married again . . . happily this time. I still cared about

my career, but that wasn't the most important thing. My *life* was. Isn't that wild? It was like my life was so perfect. I had what I wanted. I went to work and I felt good—and successful. They didn't give me a hard time about being pregnant; they were excited for me. It was as if nothing could touch me, nothing could go wrong. Wow, I want to do this again! I wonder what else could happen.

We each got a letter from Elizabeth about six months later. Actually, it was a wedding announcement. She wrote exuberantly about how she had met, fallen in love with, and married Ben. Shortly after, she got a promotion and transferred with her husband to the country where she had wanted to live.

For Elizabeth, the visualization exercise put her in touch with what she wanted for herself personally and professionally. She realized that her job was important and that she valued being recognized for her contribution, but she also realized that her personal life required attention. Elizabeth had been focusing so much on work that she seemed almost shocked to realize that there were other important motivators in her life. She began to explore the possibility that she could experience happiness and fulfillment through marriage and motherhood in addition to her work relationship. Once she had visualized these possibilities, she felt secure in pursuing them.

Elizabeth then began making choices that closed the gaps between her pictures (vision) and her reality. She used visualization as a catalyst to get her life back on the right track. Elizabeth is a woman who has decided to live "choicefully" so that she can get what she wants out of life. She has been willing to sacrifice who she was for who she could become.

Visualization: Finding Out What You Really Want

The things you dream, imagine, and long for constitute your best self. By following the technique we outline next, you will create a refreshed and refined picture—a vision—of how you want your life to be. Once you have this vision clearly embla-zoned in your mind, we'll take you through the steps to help you make it a reality.

Getting Started

To begin, you need to schedule some private time for your-self—an hour or so—with no interruptions. Go to a place that makes you feel comfortable, safe, and relaxed—perhaps a spe-cial place in your home, or somewhere outside, such as on a beach, in a forest, or on a hillside.

As you prepare for this luxury, you should start to feel a lit-tle rush of excitement and glimmer of anticipation. You're doing something private and special just for yourself. For a few hours, you'll set aside stress and tension, and feel rejuvenated and re-freshed. You'll be awash in the possibilities of the best your life can be. To set the mood, you may want to play some soothing music—something to provide a gentle background for your thoughts. Whatever it takes for you to relax, we urge you to do it. (If you find that you can't get in the mood, take a break for a while. Don't force it, or you'll ruin the experience.)

The warm-up passages that follow were written to help you create your vision. There are several ways to use them:

- Read through all of the passages; then get comfortable and let your thoughts flow as you mentally guide your-self.
- Ask someone close to you to help by slowly leading you through the visualization passages. If you take turns, you can share your ideas and dreams.
- Make a personal tape by recording the passages so that you can practice this technique whenever you want to.

There is no need to write your thoughts down as you're vi-sioning; it is more important to flow through the entire process. Don't be alarmed if you don't get a clear image. Some women see things in vibrant detail; others just sort of think about it. Since this is a technique that gets easier with practice, we'll start you out with some warm-up passages.

Visioning Warm-Ups

With your eyes closed, concentrate on relaxing. Breathe deeply in and out, and blow away all current thoughts and concerns. With each breath, you become more relaxed. You feel the relaxation spreading through the muscles in your head and behind your eyes. The comfort washes down your neck and your shoulders, through your spine. You continue breathing deeply, and your legs begin to relax and feel weightless. Your feet and your hands are so relaxed you almost can't tell that they're there.

Imagine the feeling you get when you're snuggled into your bed in the morning just before you get up. You're groggy and warm and rested, and you're trying to remember the wonderful dream you were just having. You can't quite remember. You feel as if you're just about to wake up.

For a moment, you forget who you are and where you are. You look at the calendar on the wall, and it's three years from now. It's hard to believe . . . let's see, on your last birthday, you were how old? You look at your comfortable surroundings. What do you see? Where are you? Are you with anyone?

You smile as you count your blessings. You've got your health, you're happy, and you're successful. You've never felt better in your life! And you're excited about the week ahead. You've got three really important things to do this week. They are . . .

It's time to get up and get into your daily routine. You get ready for work, and on your way out the door, you take one last look in the mirror. You like what you see—your hair, your clothes, your smile, your own look.

You get to your office . . . ahhh, here it is. You look lovingly at the familiar surroundings, the mementos of the last few years. You smile and open your calendar; today is a pretty typical day. Who will you see? What will you do? You immerse yourself in the joy of having finally created a work relationship that meets your needs. You marvel at how it has all worked out. You like what you're doing and who you are doing it with. You like the way you feel—the sense of accomplishment and contribution. Time flies . . . and it's time to leave your work behind.

You're very excited about this evening. What are you doing? What are you thinking? How does it feel?

It's been a wonderful day, and you're relaxed and ready to go to sleep. As you're getting ready for bed, you hear a noise coming from your living area. You go to check, and you find an old friend who has come to visit you. As you approach her, she smiles. You see the resemblance, yet you see the differences in each other too. It's amazing! It's you! It's the you from three years ago. You're so happy she's here! There are so many things you want to tell her about your journey. You have so much to share. You want to thank her for . . . You want to encourage her to . . . And, you want to reassure her that . . .

You're tired. You hug her. She's so glad to have come. She'll let herself out. You go to bed content and joyful. And you rest.

Reflection

How did it go? Were you surprised? Was it easy for you? If so, jot down those things (i.e., location, time of day, music) that made it easy for you so that you can create that same environment when you use visualization in the future.

If you had a hard time getting started or relaxing, jot down
what you will do differently the next time so that you will be
more effective:

_____

_____

_____

Now that you've taken this time for yourself, we recommend that you capture the energy of your experience: Describe
what happened using language in the present tense, and share
your vision with someone close to you, talking as if your vision
is happening right now. To help with this exercise, answer the
following questions regarding your vision (use the present
tense):

In your vision, what are you doing? How are you spending
your day and evening?

I am_____

_____

_____

_____

_____

_____

_____

_____

What are the relationships you value? Consider the three spheres
of work, personal and social. Who is in your life, and why?

I'm with_____

_____

_____

_____

_____

How are you feeling? What signals is your body sending you?
How do you feel emotionally in response to what you're doing?
Are you happy? excited? peaceful?

I feel _____

_____

_____

_____

_____

_____

What does this experience tell you about your own values and
beliefs? What are you learning?

I value_____

_____

_____

_____

_____

_____

I believe _____

_____

_____

_____

I am learning_____

_____

_____

_____

_____

   This is your vision of your best self. The clearer your vision is, the easier it is to become what you envision. By capturing your thoughts on paper, you'll better understand the choices available to you. By sharing your vision with others, you'll garner support for the changes you want to make. Focus on the positive things you were doing, and you'll be motivated to action. Reflect on the positive feelings you experienced, and they will reinforce your actions. Think about what you wrote under the headings "I value," "I believe," and "I am learning" because it illuminates those values and beliefs that are the foundation for your life. They are the driving forces behind the needs you have and the behaviors you exhibit. Embrace them and you will know how to make choices that don't compromise your integrity.

   With repeated effort, you can become increasingly adept at using your mind as a window to your soul. Visualization is a skill that will help you set goals and get clarity around the issues in your life that you want to resolve.

The Work Relationship

   The next exercise focuses your thoughts on the work relationship you are striving to improve. If you have already made some decisions about this relationship in the warm-up exercises, use the next exercise to fine-tune your ideas and images.

   Using what you learned in the warm-up, find a way to put yourself in your most relaxed state. Close your eyes, and concentrate on relaxing your mind and your body so that you are open to new possibilities. Breathe deep breaths in and out. Relax your forehead, your jaw, your neck, and your shoulders. Let a wave of relaxation flow over your chest and out your arms and fingertips. Feel your stomach muscles relax. Notice as your lower back becomes unstrained and relaxed. Continue breathing deeply as you relax your legs and feet. Get comfortable, and visualize a work relationship that works for you:

Think about the future. Think about starting the day in the best way possible. Even though it is a *work* day, you're excited about what's ahead of you. You took responsibility for your work relationship some time ago, and since then, things have changed. Now you have a work relationship that meets your needs. Once you decided to take action, you've found that it is possible to get what you want.

As you finish getting ready for the day, you smile at your reflection in the mirror. Boy, do you look good! Now that you're not stressed about your work relationship, you look younger, your weight is where you want it to be, you're able to wear the clothes you want to wear. You stop for a moment and take it all in.

It's amazing how going to work is no longer a chore. The environment is different. Where are you working now? Where is it located? What does your work space look like? What are the mementos of your accomplishments and relationships?

As you talk with people at work, there's an excitement in the air. This is a very special day for you; tonight there's going to be a celebration in your honor. All the people who really matter to you will be there. It's such a special event that you've decided to take the afternoon off so that you can enjoy getting ready for it. You want to look and feel your best because you've been waiting for this moment for a long time. You've dreamed about being recognized for your work accomplishments and for who you are as an individual. Tonight those dreams will come true. And because your friends and associates know you so well, they've planned the perfect way to celebrate. What will it be? A big gala or a small intimate affair? Who will be there?

It's now time for the event. You walk in and are

greeted by the smiling faces of the people you work with and your friends and loved ones. They're all there together. They tell you that you look great. They talk about how much you mean to them . . . about how proud they are of your accomplishments. Who do you see and what are they saying? Who have you known for a long time? And who is relatively new in your life? What are you being praised for? How do you feel?

As you watch this wonderful evening unfold, you have some private thoughts of your own. You're thinking about the choices you made and the goals you set. You're reflecting on the decisions you made about what was really important to you—in work and in life . . . the values and beliefs that you were unwilling to compromise on. They are . . .

You're thinking about how you took a troubled work relationship and turned it into one that works for you. You had to change some things. What were they? Which relationships did you keep and improve? Were there any that you were compelled to leave behind? Why? What have you learned? What has surprised you? What have you known all along?

This really is a time of celebration. It's wonderful to see all the people who are important to you in one room. You realize that you've made all of this happen. You knew what you wanted, and you pursued it. It wasn't always easy, but you persevered. Now it's time to congratulate yourself, inside, quietly, privately. You realize that it's really what you think about yourself that matters the most. So you give yourself an invisible hug, and celebrate what you've become. You did it!

Capturing the Vision

In the preceding exercise, you intuitively led yourself to where you really want to go. These mental images and ideas can become a clear target to guide you as you make decisions about the work relationship you truly want to have. At the same time, you've glimpsed how this work relationship fits into the rest of your life. While it's still fresh in your mind, capture your vision on paper and refer to it often as you begin making smart choices for your future. As you reflect on your vision, answer these questions (in the present tense):

What is your work environment like (formal or casual; friendly or competitive; personal mementos; view; etc.)? Where is it located (in your home? in an office building? which city? etc.)?

_____

_____

_____

What does your work environment tell you about what you value?

_____

_____

_____

What are the relationships you value in the three spheres of work, personal, and social? Indicate the relationships you've had for a long time and those that are new. Think about who is in your life and why.

I'm with_____

_____

_____

_____

_____

_____

_____

_____

_____

_____

What have you accomplished, and what does it mean to you?
Why are you being praised?

_____

_____

_____

_____

_____

What are you congratulating yourself for? What means the
most to you?

_____

_____

_____

_____

_____

What does this experience tell you about what you value and
truly believe?

_____

_____

_____

_____

_____

What will have to change for you to make this vision a reality?

_____

_____

_____

_____

_____

_____

Now that you've captured your vision and its meaning on paper, continue to reflect on it as you contemplate the choices you are making. Many successful women carry their written vision and belief statements in their daily planners or post them on the wall as a reminder and reference. In this way, they continue to be clear about what they truly want so that they can make appropriate choices. It's also helpful to share your vision with loved ones to enroll their support in helping you achieve your vision.

Visualization is a skill, and it becomes easier with time. The beauty of it is that you can take it anywhere and do it almost any time. Using visualization regularly will help you relax and unleash the truest part of yourself. For now, spend some time reflecting on what you visioned and why. This will help you create internal momentum for the choices you'll be asked to make in the next chapter.

6

Celebrate or Take Off the Hat

The two important things [I have learned are] that you are as powerful and strong as you allow yourself to be, and that the most difficult part of any endeavor is taking the first step, making the first decision.

Robyn Davidson, in *Meditations for Women
Who Do Too Much*

It's now time to take the first step and make the first decision. Armed with your vision of your best self, you are prepared to make your choice: stay in your relationship and be happy, or leave it and be happy. We are reminded of a cartoon picturing a grumpy-faced man wearing a party hat, surrounded by revelers, with his wife looking on and saying: "Either cheer up or take off the hat!" The same message goes for you. If you're unhappy in your work relationship, then get out, or change it. If you're going to stay, figure out how you can make that a situation worth celebrating. The worst choice is to stay stuck, wearing all the right clothes but feeling none of the excitement.

You have considerable control over the status of your work relationship. The key to exercising that control is to know what you want by first creating a mental picture (vision) and then having the courage to create the work relationship of your dreams. In Chapter 5, you developed a vision. In this chapter you'll learn to make choices around that vision.

In our discussions about choices, we frequently use terms such as *do, think, feel,* and *your body's reaction.* According to a prominent theory in human behavior called control theory, "Our behavior is made up of four individual components: acting [doing], thinking, feeling, and the concurrent physiology, all of which always blend together to make a whole or total behavior. . . . We have nowhere near the quick or arbitrary control over our feelings and/or our physiology as we have over our actions and thoughts."[1] Based on this theory, it is in the thinking, and specifically in the doing, that we conjure the power to create change in our work relationships. In other words, if you want to change your work relationship, focus on your thoughts and your actions.

This is not to discount the significance of feelings and your body's reactions. As women, we take great pride in our ability to feel and get frustrated when people tell us to stop being emotional or sensitive. Our feelings and our body's reactions can be natural indicators that something just isn't right for us. Remember Sue from Chapter 3 who took three aspirin at the beginning and end of each work day? What was her body telling her—and did she get the message? Still, your physical reactions and your feelings don't create the change. It is your commitment to do something to alter these alarming body cues and signals that creates change. For example, if you begin setting clear boundaries around what is acceptable to you in your work relationship and you communicate and clarify your boundaries to key people in this relationship, then the context of the relationship has already changed. This change will eventually affect how you feel. You'll notice your feelings shift from those of frustration to those of relief, and any unpleasant physical symptoms will often retreat as well.

Experience, the Best Teacher

A core premise of this book is that women create work relationships that mirror the stages of personal relationships. Therefore,

the emotional reactions we experience when our work relationships are troubled and failing are similar to those we experience
when our intimate relationships are troubled or ending. Let's
take an example from a common experience that we have all
had in our personal lives.

Remember your first broken heart? Recall how you felt:
miserable, alone, rejected, insecure, afraid, unattractive, angry.
Does this ring any bells? What were your first thoughts initially
after the breakup? Some common thoughts are, "I'll never love
anyone this much again! I will never get over this! Why does it
have to hurt so bad! I was a fool!" Recall how your body responded: "I lost so much weight I couldn't eat or keep anything
down." Or, "I gained fifteen pounds because all I did was eat,
eat, eat." "I had headaches all the time." "I couldn't sleep."
Now remember some of the positive changes you made when
you got past your grieving period: "I lost weight," "I changed
my look," "I went out on blind dates," "I went out with my
friends," "I got involved in my work," "I got my own job making my own money." Notice that all of these statements are action oriented.

Your healing process occurred when you started thinking
differently and doing the work to get past that relationship.
That's when you started to open up and venture into new relationships. You learned that moping around being miserable
only made you feel worse. You also realized that other people
started getting tired of your "he done me wrong" song. You
learned that you could heal from the pain only by getting out
there again. In fact, you grew and learned from your mistakes.
You may have fallen in and out of love several times since then.
You simply picked up the pieces, learned the key lessons, and
moved on.

It's the same process with work relationships. How many
times have you felt miserable, angry, or humiliated about events
that occurred in your work relationship? Remember when you
were discounted at a meeting in front of your peers and you
just wanted to scream? Or, you weren't told about a significant
event or meeting for the umpteenth time, and while the
umpteenth apology was being offered, you felt as if you were
about to break down and cry from anger. Or, you were passed

up for that promotion, and you felt depressed and even physically ill.

To get out of that quagmire, you ultimately changed how you thought about yourself, and you began establishing boundaries. You began to change the nature of your work relationship. You learned to give clear feedback, set and clarify expectations, and enroll people to support you. Your *actions*, not your *feelings*, got you through the rough spots.

You are not a victim of your troubled work relationship; you have the power and the control to change it. You have three choices:

1. *Stay and be happy.* Decide that your principles, values, and beliefs are aligned closely enough with your organization's so that you can have a rewarding work relationship where you are. You'll need to take some action steps to get all of your needs met, but overall, you think it can be done.

This was the choice of Betty, in Chapter 1, who "married" the Health Care Organization. Recall that she had reached a crossroads when her company began reorganizing and downsizing, and she witnessed some questionable treatment of her coworkers. She had also grown tired of a relentless travel schedule that kept her away from her family. Throughout all of this, she weighed the pros and cons and decided that the work relationship was important enough to her to continue to strive for improvement. Through her results on the job and the support of her sponsor, ultimately she was able to improve her work relationship to better accommodate her personal needs.

Another example is the case of Kate, the choiceful mistress. She found temporary solace in a compromise position where her employer pays for her schooling while she continues to contribute to the company's objectives. Kate readily admits that ultimately she will have to make a choice to leave her work relationship behind to pursue her dreams, but, for now, she has chosen to stay and be happy.

2. *Leave and be happy.* Decide that there are irreconcilable differences between you and your work relationship partner(s). Your values, beliefs, principles, or dreams are not consistent

enough with theirs to keep you in the relationship. It is time for you to move on and get your needs met elsewhere.

Think of Sharon and her work relationship with Bright Company. As soon as her new boss started treating her disrespectfully in regard to her motherhood, she knew that a fundamental line had been crossed. The conflict was chiefly between her and this one individual manager, so she shared her story with other managers, hoping to get their support. They appeared sympathetic, but no one took action on her behalf. Although she had experienced a fulfilling ten-year relationship with Bright, there was no way that she would compromise her principles to keep an intolerable work relationship. It took Sharon no more than six months to make a decision and terminate her work relationship. She's sorry that Bright didn't fight to keep her, but, as she says, "I won, and my family won. I'm happy, and I'm also a lot smarter now."

3. *Do nothing and choose misery.* Choosing misery is deciding to do nothing and continue with the status quo, even if the relationship is causing you pain. This choice does not put you in effective control, but it must meet some of your needs or you wouldn't choose it.

Consider the story of Sandy, the reluctant mistress. She's been choosing misery since she got turned down for an assignment in Ted's organization. Although we can argue that her feelings of betrayal are well justified, she's remaining stuck in an unfulfilling work relationship. She's fermenting animosity for Ted and choosing to stay in a state of confusion and frustration. Her current choices will not help her create the work relationship she really wants.

The first two choices—stay or leave—are about taking responsibility for yourself and doing something to create the work relationship that you want. You'll choose the stage of work relationship that's best for you—that is, Married, Fiancée, Mistress, Girlfriend, or Dating—by determining how it fits within the context of your organization's needs and its congruency with your values, beliefs, and principles. What's important is that you will have chosen to pursue a more satisfying work relationship, with the same organization or a new one.

The third choice, misery, is about allowing things to happen to you versus your being the master of what happens. In choosing misery, you abdicate your responsibility and control to someone or something else. You are stuck and choose to stay stuck. Because this is such a disconcerting choice, we've written more about below. You may want to read on even if you're pretty clear about the decision you want to make.

Choosing Misery

It's not our intent to be harsh or insensitive if you're stuck; we've both been there. It *is* our intent to increase your awareness that misery is a *choice* that you make for yourself. Rather than experiencing the exhilaration of taking action to correct a troubled relationship, you find yourself ruminating over and over again about what you should do but "can't," and you end up doing nothing. After a while, even your best friends get tired of the subject.

Doing nothing can go on for a long time. Unfortunately, there's a sizable group of women who *appear* permanently stuck. We say "appear" because we don't believe anyone is permanently stuck. We feel you choose to be stuck as long as it meets your needs. Our interviews have consistently shown that the longer a woman is stuck in an unfulfilling work relationship, the more embittered she becomes, and the more she loses her self-esteem. If it goes on too long, it becomes a no-win situation, and eventually either you or your organization will move to dislodge you from your stuck state. If it's done by your organization, it could come to an end with a request for your resignation or an outright termination. If you wait too long to leave on your own, you may not have much confidence left with which to build a new relationship.

You might be wondering why anyone would choose to be miserable. Well, you don't overtly say, "I'm choosing to be miserable." You covertly "do" misery, most of the time via the game of intellectualization. Most of us have become very proficient at this game, a way of anesthetizing the pain. We can out-think our way through every situation or challenge. We're masters at it and use this cognitive ability to justify our willingness to tolerate an intolerable work relationship. We can think things are good even when reality clearly shows they're not. Thus, we intellectualize our misery by using fear stoppers.

Fear Stoppers

A fear stopper is the excuse used to stay in a bad work relationship. It is a defense mechanism that can prevent you from dealing with the dissonance created by the distance between your pictures and your reality. Which of the following classic fear stoppers could be keeping you stuck in misery?

- *"I don't deserve/I'm not good enough."* "I don't deserve to have the supportive work relationship I've dreamed of anyway. I haven't worked hard enough to have it. I'm not good enough." Your fear is that maybe you don't deserve a quality work relationship that nourishes and sustains you.
- *"I know how bad this is."* "At least I know how bad this is. I don't know what it's like somewhere else. I know it isn't right; I'm not happy. But at least I know how miserable this relationship is, and I know how to deal with it. I'd better stick with this because I don't know what the next relationship will be like." Your fear of change and the unknown is so strong that choosing misery seems more appealing than the unknown.
- *"Will someone else ever want me?"* "I'm damaged goods. No organization will want me. Since I failed at one work relationship, I'm less marketable. Everyone will know I'm a failure." You lack confidence and question your abilities. Your fear is rejection and wondering if you can compete.
- *"I just don't fit."* "I'm not able to fit into this work relationship. I really don't have what it takes." This fear is tied to thinking and feeling that you lack the political fi-

nesse, intellectual prowess, and organizational savvy to create and sustain a dynamic work relationship.

- *"I don't know how."* "I just don't know how to do work relationships. I don't like the small talk, the politics." This is similar to the "I don't fit" fear stopper in that you don't believe you're quite smooth enough or skilled enough to play the game. You find it threatening, so you admit defeat before you even try.
- *"I don't have a plan."* "I don't know what I really want to do. I don't have all the answers right now." You fear making a mistake and being unable to control the outcome, so you simply don't define a plan.

By choosing misery, you do not take effective control of your life or career. If you're experiencing any one of these fear stoppers, you need to stop and ask yourself a few questions:

What is my greatest fear?_____

_____

_____

What is my fear shielding me from?_____

_____

_____

What are the benefits to me of choosing misery? What am I getting out of it?_____

_____

_____

Continue to reflect on why you may be continuing to choose misery. Once you understand the needs you are trying to get met, you may find other ways to fulfill them instead of choosing misery. We invite you to consider other options by taking the Choice Quiz now.

Ready to "Do Choice"?

The Choice Quiz, shown as Figure 6-1, helps you reaffirm the choice you've already made. Or if you are still vacillating, it will reveal the direction you really want to take. Answer the questions truthfully, picking the one choice that fits you best.

Figure 6-1. The Choice Quiz: I love it, I love it not.

Answer these 10 questions truthfully. Pick the one answer that fits you best.

1. My current work relationship is not what I want, but:
    a. _____ It's better than nothing. (1)
    b. _____ I feel it's workable now that I'm clearer. (2)
    c. _____ There's no "but"; I want out. (3)

2. The current economic climate with layoffs and downsizing makes me feel as if:
    a. _____ I should count my blessings and hang in with this relationship. (1)
    b. _____ I should work harder to improve upon what I have. (2)
    c. _____ It's not the best time to leave, but even with that, I know I can't stay. (3)

3. The thought of really ending this work relationship:
    a. _____ Is immobilizing for me. I can't get past my fears. (1)
    b. _____ Makes me question if I've done all I could and should have to make it work. (2)
    c. _____ Is freeing. I feel that it's time to leave. (3)

4. In general, ending a relationship is:
    a. _____ Easy for me once I get focused. (3)
    b. _____ Hard, but if it's right, I'll do it. (2)
    c. _____ Almost impossible for me to initiate or do. (1)

5. My closest friend has repeatedly told me:
    a. _____ "Be very sure it's really what you want to do." (2)
    b. _____ "No job is worth what you're going through. Leave, and you'll land on your feet." (3)
    c. _____ "Realize there's good and bad in every work relationship. That's how life is. Somewhere else isn't going to be any better." (1)

6. My decision to stay or leave has to be factored in with other critical considerations, such as:
   a. _____ My family, who depend on me. I can't do just what's right for me; I have to consider other people. (1)
   b. _____ There are no elements more critical than my own happiness. (3)
   c. _____ The void it would leave in the project I'm working on and the company. (2)

7. Leaving this work relationship would signify:
   a. _____ They won. They got me out. (1)
   b. _____ I won. I chose to leave and did it. (2)
   c. _____ No one wins or loses. (3)

8. When I'm thinking clearly about what to do with this work relationship:
   a. _____ My body responds wildly with headaches, backaches, or sweats; or it shuts down completely and I sleep all the time. (1)
   b. _____ My body feels so serene and peaceful. It's as if a load had been lifted off my shoulders. (3)
   c. _____ My body reaction vacillates from responding serenely to breaking down. (2)

9. If I left, people would say:
   a. _____ "Good; she's gone." (1)
   b. _____ "We should have tried harder to keep her." (2)
   c. _____ "She did what was best for her." (3)

10. My concern level about what people at work would say about my leaving is:
    a. _____ Zilch—zero! I don't care how they feel. How I feel is most important. (3)
    b. _____ High. I don't want them to affect my reputation adversely. I've gotten paranoid. (1)
    c. _____ Moderate. I hope they say truthful things. You never know if I'll need to come back or work with them again. (2)

Scoring the Choice Quiz

Now total the numbers in the parentheses after each response that you checked to derive your total score. Then interpet it:

Score	Interpretation
1–10	You're choosing misery. You are stuck and aren't living choicefully. Consider, "What will it take for me to move on?"
11–20	Your focus is to stay, make it work, and be happy. You still have an emotional attachment.
21–30	Leave and be happy. You're less emotionally attached and have started the separation process. You need to find your happiness elsewhere.

It's choice time. Which one is it?

[ ] I've chosen misery because:_____

_____

_____

_____

[ ] I've chosen to stay and be happy because:_____

_____

_____

_____

[ ] I've chosen to leave and be happy because:_____

_____

_____

_____

If you're still choosing misery, it's because it's the best way you know how to handle the situation at the moment. Keep asking yourself what you are getting out of this choice so that you can determine what will have to change in order for you to choose to stay or leave and be happy. If you've made it through the crossroads with a clear choice, then you're ready to start making some smart moves. Turn the page and get started!

Part IV
Getting Past Go

To love what you do and feel that it matters—how could anything be more fun?

Katherine Graham, in *Great Quotes from Great Women*

Choices are liberating. Now you can channel all your energy into living the way you really want to—doing those things that matter to you and having fun along the way. Say good-bye to misery, fear, and doubt, and hello to life and all the wonders that are yours to discover.

In Part IV, you will establish a game plan for living out your choices. You'll learn specific techniques and strategies to either stay and be happy or leave and be happy. Chapter 7 is full of opportunities for you to learn the do's and don'ts of making Smart Moves from Smart Women who've been through the same process you're now going through. These ten Smart Moves cover everything: positioning support networks, negotiations, handling objections, and more. By tailoring these moves to fit your own situation, you'll be ready to develop a road map to success in Chapter 8. Since you're likely to encounter some resistance from others to your plan, we've also included some situational exercises that prepare you to handle any of the emotional reactions others could have to your choices.

7

Smart Moves

> My philosophy is that not only are you responsible for your
> life, but doing the best at this moment puts you in the best
> place for the next moment.
>
> Oprah Winfrey, in *Do It!*

Now that you've made your choice, your next challenge is to
figure out the best way to pursue your dream and make it a reality. Our own experience is that this is where you begin to feel
as if you're working without a safety net. You're leaving the security of the known for the uncertainty of the future. You're out
to create your own world and shape your own reality, but you
may not have a clue about where to begin.

When we found ourselves at this juncture, our impulses
were to reach out for help, advice, and comfort from others. We
knew what we wanted to do; we just weren't sure how to go
about it. So we began asking questions of other women who
had embarked on an odyssey to change their work relationship:

"Did you feel as if you were going crazy?"
"How did you know it was time to leave?"
"Why did you decide to stay?"
"How did you negotiate for what you wanted?"
"Are you happier now?"
"Is the grass really greener on the other side?"

Sometimes we got intriguing answers, and sometimes we just created more questions. We didn't have the full picture, but we were beginning to put the pieces of the puzzle together.

We talked to each other about what we were going through: the politics of leaving, the loss of relationships we thought would last, our fear of making the wrong moves. We shared bits and pieces of wisdom we'd gleaned from other women. We laughed and cried over what we had learned the hard way, stubbing our toes as we stumbled through the transitions in our work lives. Then an interesting thing happened: Once we started talking to people about the choices we had made and the dreams we had for ourselves, we started getting calls from other women who were struggling with the same work relationship issues. Our discussions all posed the same question: How do you create and sustain a fulfilling work relationship? Our quest for the best answer to that question became the genesis of this book.

Not content to rely solely on our own experiences, we began interviewing women who had answered the question in a variety of ways. We spoke with women who had stayed with their organizations and put renewed energy into their existing work relationships. We talked with others who had left unsatisfactory relationships so they could forge new ones elsewhere. And we pursued the candid confessions of women who were stuck in the valley between staying and leaving feeling miserable, and offering advice about what not to do.

We wove all of this knowledge into a tapestry of do's and don'ts for women eager to improve their work relationships and their lives in general. We offer this learning to you in the form of ten Smart Moves. Regardless of whether you stay or leave, these Smart Moves position you in the best place for the next phase in your life.

Ten Smart Moves

These moves are flexible enough to fit any situation. We've numbered them to get you started, but you can use a menu approach to put them together in any order that works for you. The key is to make sure that you have a plan that incorporates all ten Smart Moves to ensure your success. As you review each one, think of how they will support the choice you made in Chapter 6.

Smart Move 1: Own Your Choice

> When you make up your mind, Providence moves in your direction. When I said what I wanted and people knew that the discussion was over, then they started doing everything they could to support me. All kinds of things started happening and appearing that I wouldn't have seen before.
>
> Janet Reid, interviewee

Now that you've made your choice, own it. Don't relinquish your power to anyone else to decide what's right for you. There's a lot of talk today about empowerment. Many women think, incorrectly, that empowerment is something that is given to them, not something they do for themselves. Why wait around for somebody else to give you power? Your power lies within you. Grab the reins and hold on.

Make sure that your actions and behaviors are consistent with the choices you have made. For example, if you have decided to stay in your current work relationship and improve it, then stop complaining about it and start sharing a plan with your organization to improve things. If you've decided to let your relationship go, then stop putting your energies into trying to fix it, and start polishing up your résumé and getting yourself energized to create a more rewarding relationship with a new organization or your own business. If you say one thing and then do another, people won't take you seriously.

We recommend that you make a pact with yourself to own your choices. It's simple, but it confirms your commitment and keeps you from waffling too much as you execute your choices. Start by filling in the blanks on the form that follows:

Promises to Myself

(date:_____)

From this day forward, I promise myself to behave in a manner consistent with my choice to_____(stay in/leave) my current work relationship. As evidence of my commitment to create the best work relationship I can, I will do the following:

Start (behaviors)   Stop (behaviors)
[e.g., making a plan]   [e.g.,   talking
                                          about it]

Keep in mind that your behaviors demonstrate to others that you are taking effective control of your life. Actions do speak louder than words. If you live your life choicefully, the result is that others will respect your choices and acknowledge your right to pursue them.

Smart Move 2: Feed the Source

If you could once make up your mind never to undertake more work than you can carry on calmly, quietly, without hurry or flurry and if the instant you feel yourself growing nervous and out of breath, you would stop and take breath, you would find this simple commonsense rule doing for you what no prayers or tears could ever accomplish.

Elizabeth Prentiss, in *Women, Heroes, and a Frog*

We are often so busy taking care of everyone else's needs that we neglect our own. If you realized in Chapter 4 that your life is out of balance and you are receiving danger signals from your own body and from other people, stop and remember to feed the source. This means that you take a personal time out and administer first aid to yourself. It's just like the announcement at the beginning of every plane flight: "First put the mask on yourself, and then assist your child." In your case, aid may come in the form of a brief vacation, a daily walk, a few hours in a movie theater—anything that refreshes you. Only by keeping yourself healthy and strong can you summon the strength to support yourself and those you care about.

There are several reasons that Feeding the Source is such a Smart Move for today's working woman. Consider just a few of these issues and trends that could apply to you:

• *The sandwich generation.* Are you part of the generation of women who are sandwiched in the middle with responsibilities to care for both young children and aging parents, all the while balancing a career and striving to get your own needs met? If so, you've experienced firsthand how important it is to keep your own well from running dry.

• *Increasing health risks.* Do you tend to take your body for granted, thinking that it will do whatever you want it to do whenever you want it to do it? Unfortunately, research shows that many working women ignore their bodies, only to discover that they shouldn't have taken their health for granted. As personal stress increases, so does the incidence of infertility, heart disease, and cancer. Diseases that were once thought to be the purview of working men are now hounding working women. Also consider that the physiology that protects women during childbearing years plays catch-up at menopause. During the next two decades, 40 to 50 million baby-boom women will undergo menopause, placing them at higher risk for heart disease and other ailments.[1] Now is the time to take care of your health.

• *Keepers of the flame.* Have you achieved a level of professional success well beyond that of your predecessors, only to feel honor-bound to carry the torch for current and future generations? Do you feel that your actions become the acid test of whether others who follow will be granted similar opportunities in your company or organization? If so, you are one of the pioneers, the keepers of the flame, the ones who will create the changes that will benefit all women. It is a very seductive role—and an exhausting one. We hear from many women who are tired of being "the one"—the one female at an executive level, the one Black, Hispanic, or Asian woman to reach a certain rung on the corporate ladder. This becomes a tremendous burden, especially when women deny their own needs because of their perceived responsibility to advance the cause of all women. If this rings a bell for you, you need to ask yourself: "Who is supporting me? In my efforts to win this battle, will I lose control over my own life? Am I rallying other people to support the cause so I don't have to do it all alone? Where will *my* strength come from?" Realize that you must have a plan to take care of your own needs.

• *Learning and healing time.* Do you ever feel that you need some time to slow down and reflect on everything that has happened to you? to consider what you've learned? to heal from the wounds you receive every day? Everyone needs quiet time. This will become increasingly important for you as you do the hard work to bring your choices to life.

Jot down how you will take care of your own needs. Think about those things that bring you peace, that comfort you, that give you strength: a bubble bath, a movie, an invigorating workout, a week in the Bahamas, a romantic rendezvous away from the kids, a sabbatical. Write down here how you will "feed the source":

_____

_____

_____

You may want to go back to your "Promises to Myself" contract on page 112. Add the behaviors that you are going to start doing to take care of yourself. Make a specific request of your family and friends to ask about your progress from time to time.

Smart Move 3: Visualize Your Choice

One morning you will awake to find that you are the person you dreamed of—doing what you wanted to do—simply because you had the courage to believe in your potential and hold on to your dream.

Donna Levine

You've made your choice to stay or to leave, but do you have a clear mental picture of exactly what this choice means to you? Remember the visualization technique you used in Chapter 5 to conjure up the image of what you want your life to be like. Now is the time to clarify that vision so that you have a clear picture of the choices you're making and can take action to accomplish the goals you set for yourself.

First consider the wealth of exciting options available to you now. Select your choice from the list of options that correspond to your commitment to stay or to leave:

Staying Options

- Stay in the same relationship and improve it.
- Stay as long as the relationship meets my conditions.
- Stay with my company or organization but negotiate for a new boss or a new assignment.
- Stay but work part-time.

Leaving Options

- Leave to spend time with my family.
- Leave to pursue an advanced education, skill, or degree.
- Leave to become more successful at another company or organization where I can create the work relationships I want and need.
- Leave to start my own business as an entrepreneur.
- Leave to go on a sabbatical—travel, take time off to rest and heal.
- Leave immediately, even without a thorough plan—I can't stand it any longer!

Think about what will have to happen to make this choice a reality by answering the questions below:

What needs am I trying to get met by making this choice (e.g., freedom, financial gain, family issues, personal fulfillment, skill enhancement)?_____

_____

How does my vision allow for balance of my personal, social, and work spheres?_____

_____

What relationship stage do I need to be in to get my needs met (Fiancée, Mistress, etc.)?_____

If I've chosen to have a work relationship, what parameters or boundaries do I need to establish (e.g., number of hours I'm willing to work, types of assignments, travel, pay)?_____

_____

_____

If I've chosen not to have a work relationship, what do I need to include in my vision to ensure personal fulfillment (e.g., starting a family, getting more education, participating in community events or volunteer work)?_____

_____

_____

Keeping these answers in mind, pause to reflect on your mental picture of your choice. You should feel excited and passionate about your vision. This is important because your vision provides the foundation for your plan and seals your commitment to your choice. If you can see it, you can make it so. For now, think about it, refine it in your mind, and own it. We'll help you formulate a concrete plan in the next chapter.

Smart Move 4: Get Support

Trouble is a part of life, and if you don't share it, you don't give the person who loves you a chance to love you enough.

Dinah Shore, in *Quotable Women*

Support comes from friends, family, and coworkers who help you follow through on your decisions. But support can be tricky. If you rely too much on the support of other people, you can find yourself having a hard time wrestling your life back from them. If you don't let people support you enough, you'll find yourself all alone with your troubles. The key is to know what kind of support you need and who can provide it for you. Use the chart in Figure 7-1 to take a quick inventory of the supporters you already have.

As a checkpoint, ask yourself if you've identified people in each area of support at work and in your personal relationships. Do you have the same name in most of the boxes? If you do, your friends or loved ones could be feeling as if you are sucking the life right out of them. If there are voids in any of the boxes, consider who could and would support you if you asked. Remember that you don't have to do this all alone—nor should you. Just be sure to establish a network of support, not just one person.

Smart Move 5: Anticipate Emotional Reactions: Yours and Others

When someone wants you to be what you aren't or refuses you permission to be who you are, try to understand that is their problem, really, and you don't have to make it yours.

Merle Shain, *When Lovers Are Friends*

Individual change is often a polarizing event accompanied by emotionally charged behaviors. Remember that you are working to bring your mental pictures and your reality closer together. The picture you have for yourself may not be the same one that others have for you, and they may react to your actions with surprise, envy, threats, or some other behavior. They may try to manipulate you with their emotional reactions—or they may be supportive. In either case, acknowledge their feelings, but stay on course.

Keep in mind that you may be surprised by your own emotional reactions as well. If people don't respond the way you think they will, you may be slightly hurt or disappointed—or even enraged. The better prepared you are for all reactions, the

Figure 7-1. The support inventory.

Directions: Jot down the names of people who support you in your work and family relationships.

Types of Support	Work Relationships	Personal Relationships
Shield People who protect me, cover my back, watch out for me, see things I may miss that could hurt me, don't let others ridicule me in my absence.		
Mirror People who reflect back my picture of what I've said I want. They help me stay true to my best self.		
Echo Chamber People who play back what they hear me saying so I can hear it myself and make adjustments if necessary.		
Sounding Board People who understand my need to vent my frustrations without their having to reply, argue, or respond personally.		
Storyteller People who can tell stories or draw analogies so I can learn from the experiences of others.		

Jester People who can charm me out of a bad mood and encourage me to enjoy things more and laugh at myself.		
Consultant People whose advice I respect and value. They help me understand the potential consequences of choices I am making.		
Believer People who believe that I am always trying to do the right thing and support me even when I make mistakes. They remind me of my best self.		
Backer People who offer me resources to help me execute my choices. For example, they may offer me a place to stay, an airline ticket, or a loan, or they may baby-sit my children while I work.		

more smoothly you'll be able to orchestrate your Smart Moves. You've made your choice; now who out of your family (include significant other), friends, and coworkers will be supportive of that choice? Who will be unsupportive? Write down their names in the appropriate boxes in Figure 7-2. Then, in the "Notes to Myself" space, recap any trends that you see. For example, is your family supportive, but your coworkers hate your choice? Use this grid to begin thinking about the reactions you will encounter. In Chapter 8, we'll give you specific reactions you should anticipate from others depending on your choice to stay or leave.

Smart Move 6: Make Time Your Ally

> Some things . . . arrive on their own mysterious hour, on their own terms and not yours, to be seized or relinquished forever.
>
> Gail Godwin, in *Quotable Women*

Have you ever planned everything out to perfection, then nothing happened as planned—but it all worked out anyway?

Figure 7-2. Anticipating emotional reactions.

Directions: In the appropriate boxes, jot down the names of people by the reactions you expect.

Reactions to My Choice	Family	Friends	Coworkers
Supportive			
Unsupportive			
Trends			
Notes to myself:			

Selecting the right time to make your move is not an exact science, but you can be strategic in your planning and conscious of factors that could benefit or sabotage your efforts. Becoming aware of all these factors will put you in a better position to negotiate for what you want. To make time your ally, begin by asking yourself, "What factors constitute good timing or bad timing for the moves I'm planning to make?" Write down all the factors you can think of. We've given you some examples to get you started:

Good Timing	Bad Timing
Company is downsizing and I could negotiate a package if I leave.	My mentor just got fired, now who will support me?
My mentor just told me that a key assignment is coming available.	The economy is in bad shape, and competition for the good jobs is fierce.

As you consider timing, determine how much emphasis you'll place on your own instincts. Trust your instincts, and when they tell you to go for it, seize the moment; when you feel that the timing is wrong, let it go. But be careful not to let timing be a fear stopper, as in "I can't leave right now; companies are laying people off. How would I ever find another job?" This is an excuse for not taking action.

Smart Move 7: Negotiate for What You Want

You cannot shake hands with a clenched fist.

Indira Gandhi, in *Great Quotes from Great Women*

Negotiation allows you to stay or leave with most of your conditions met. Preparing to negotiate helps you organize yourthoughts into a productive discussion rather than a destructive one. In this way, you can change your work relationship without damaging it or burning your bridges. There is an art to negotiation that results in creating the best possible scenario for everyone. First, you'll need to do the following:

- Get clarity on what you are negotiating for—what it looks like, what it requires.
- Understand the point of view of others in your work relationship—their needs and requirements. Consider how they will react to your proposal.
- Research and consider any precedents that have taken place in your organization relative to your situation and the relationship you are trying to forge.
- Know your legal rights and parameters if you feel you have been wronged in any way. Remember that knowledge is power.
- Rehearse "if . . . then" scenarios to prepare for any eventuality in your negotiations. For example, if you want to leave but your boss wants you to stay, then tell him that you appreciate how much he values you but that you have to do what's right for you. Perhaps offer to help him find an adequate replacement and train that person.

- Prepare yourself to be uncomfortable.
- Never threaten the other party. Keep an ace in the hole if you have one, but only hint about it.
- Be shrewd. Find a way to communicate in a way that unobtrusively makes your point.
- Practice, practice, practice. Use your support network to help you become more skilled at handling the discussion and the possible objections that may arise.

A classic sales model framework is useful for outlining your negotiations.[2] First, think about the top three critical issues you want to negotiate. Then follow the model and plug in your own words.

Summarize the situation. Begin the discussion by stating why you requested the meeting. Briefly recap the situation that has compelled you to take this action. Quickly acknowledge your understanding of the other person's needs, limitations, and opportunities.

_____

_____

_____

_____

_____

State your ideas. Clearly and succinctly state your proposal—what you want to do or accomplish.

_____

_____

_____

_____

_____

Explain how it works. Go through a logical explanation of how you see your proposal working. Paint a picture for the other person so that he or she can easily understand how it would work. Try to anticipate objections that may arise and address those objections within the context of your proposal. (Remember your "if . . . then" scenarios.)

_____

_____

_____

_____

_____

Reinforce the key benefits. Tell the other person what's in it for him or her. Explain how your proposal will benefit your relationship with him or her and with the organization.

_____

_____

_____

_____

_____

Close. When you get an indication that the other person is in agreement with your plan, in part or in total, see if he or she is ready to agree on next steps. Don't keep talking or you may talk the other person out of what you want. If the other person hasn't given you much feedback throughout the process, be sure to get a commitment at the end, such as: "If you agree to support me for this position, let's pick a date to meet with Joe and get his final approval. Would Tuesday or Wednesday work better for you?"

_____

_____

_____

In the following chapter we'll share some examples of how some Smart Women have negotiated new work relationships.

Smart Move 8: Know How to Tell Your Story

Success means not making the other person wrong.
                        Angie Thoburn, teacher and trainer

Packaging your story is important. It dovetails with other Smart Moves like soliciting support, negotiating for what you want, and managing emotional reactions. You'll need to be strategic in choosing what you tell, whom you tell, and when you tell. Otherwise, you could jeopardize your chances of getting what you want. Recognize that at some point you will have the urge to tell your story to anyone and everyone who will listen, particularly when you feel that you've been wronged or misunderstood in your work relationship. You need to know the fine art of sharing your view of your work relationship in a manner that won't cause you harm. Here's a list of tips from Smart Women who have been through the process:

- *Manage your personal intensity.* Know where your hot buttons are so that if someone pushed them, you can train yourself to step back and manage your reactions rather than be manipulated by them.
- *Understand your motivation in telling your story.* Your story should be told to help you get what you want. If you are telling it so that you can vent, lay blame, or induce guilt, there are a variety of techniques you can employ to get your needs meet without jeopardizing important relationships; for example, write a letter venting all your emotions, but don't send it.
- *Stick to the facts and the truth.* Don't embellish your story, or it will get exaggerated and come back to bite you.
- *Don't keep playing the broken record: "Poor, poor, pitiful, me."*

People will eventually grow tired of your negativity and ignore or avoid you.
- *Tell your story from an internal point of view, that is, own it: do not use an external point of view and blame others.* Own your choices—the good, the bad, and the ugly. For example, use phrases like "I chose to . . . " instead of "They made me . . . " This will build your credibility and make it easier for others to support you.
- *Tell your story in 100 words or less.* Be brief and to the point.

Smart Move 9: Have a Plan and Do It

The shortest answer is doing.

English proverb, in *Meditations for Women Who Do Too Much*

Just by reading this book and doing the exercises, you are already crafting your plan and doing it. Preparation is 80 percent of the battle. Once you've thoroughly reviewed all ten Smart Moves, we'll help you put them all together in a concise plan.

Smart Move 10: Get Centered

You can't bake a cake at 700 degrees!

Kathryn Fisher, friendly warning to author

Remember that things take time. You may wish to rush through this process, but everything will not happen exactly as you plan. Some things are simply out of your control. To have as much control as possible, focus on the areas you can influence, that excite you, and that make you feel good about yourself. Start by recalling all of the Smart Moves you've made in your life and celebrate them. Search your mind for thoughts that put everything into perspective . . . thoughts that give you peace.

If you find yourself wavering in your decision, remember that it's natural to second-guess yourself. But that's the time that you most need to center yourself again on your choices and focus on your plans. Acknowledge that you've done a lot of hard work to get to this decision. As our friend Iyanla Vanzant says: "Don't stop five minutes before the miracles!"[3]

The Ten Smart Moves in Action

Words and ideas can sound good on paper, but the test comes when they are applied to real life. To shift our discussion from the theoretical to the practical, we've included interview excerpts from two women who made their own Smart Moves. Angela, married and a mother of three, made the difficult decision to leave a good work relationship in order to pursue a dream of starting her own business. Gloria, single and career minded, steadfastly struggled with her work relationship to improve it so that her needs were met. Although their choices were different, their stories show how the ten Smart Moves helped them achieve their goals. You'll see that the order of the moves varies depending on individual circumstances but that all the moves are interrelated in some way.

For Quick Reference, they are:

1. Own Your Choice
2. Feed the Source
3. Visualize Your Choice
4. Get Support
5. Anticipate Emotional Reactions
6. Make Time Your Ally
7. Negotiate for What You Want
8. Know How to Tell Your Story
9. Have a Plan and Do It
10. Get Centered

Leaving Happy: Angela's Story

Today, Angela turned in her resignation letter. It was just a formality because everything had been worked out in advance. She'd gotten everything she wanted, and she was leaving with best wishes from key people in her organization. She couldn't believe how much support she had received. The people she cared about most at work still genuinely cared about her. She had made some significant changes in her personal and professional life. She was in a much different place than she was three years ago.

Vanessa: Angela, you spoke of your work relationship three years ago. What was going on then?

Angela: I was struggling with the decision to leave World Co. I was angry and frustrated because I had gotten so many merit increases and public accolades for my performance, but they wouldn't promote me! They kept telling me I wasn't quite ready. At the same time other people—particularly white men and women—were advancing, and they hadn't achieved half of what I'd accomplished. I felt I'd been wronged.

Vanessa: Are you suggesting there was some discrimination?

Angela: Yes, there was. It would have been hard to try to prove. But during that time black women were virtually invisible to the organization. We were clustered at entry-level positions, got the weakest assignments, and received the lowest performance ratings. We were excluded from the informal network where the real decisions were made. It wasn't easy for black women to get opportunities to develop supportive work relationships. We didn't have exposure or access to senior managers, so we didn't develop key sponsors or mentor relationships.

Vanessa: You speak of what was happening to black women as a group. How were you personally affected?

Angela: Well, three years ago I really wanted it to work. I wanted to be the example of breaking the color/sex barrier. I intended to have a close, caring work relationship. I got caught up being the first black woman to be promoted beyond the first level. Since I was the highest ranking—which, by the way, wasn't very high—I felt I had to be a role model and an inspiration to other black women. I felt so much pressure to be everything to everyone. I was the corporate civil rights crusader. I was going to get management to do the right thing by treating blacks and other people of color fairly. I asked myself, "If I can't change things, who can?"

Vanessa: It sounds like a lot was going on at work. What was going on in your personal and social life then?

Angela: It was a crazy time at home too. I unexpectedly became pregnant with our third child. I already had twin boys who were less than three years old. Unfortunately, my marriage was going through a turbulent period, and my husband wasn't prepared emotionally or financially for another child. He felt that I was not giving him enough attention and that he was competing with my job and our three kids. At work, my supervisor felt that I wasn't giving enough attention to his directives for the business. He kept telling me that I wasn't focused and had too many competing priorities. Truthfully, I didn't know if I was coming or going. At that time I despised both my husband and my boss.

Vanessa: What did you do to manage all of this?

Angela: I didn't really have a plan. I just started acting out. I threatened to divorce both my husband and my supervisor. I talked with recruiters, went on countless interviews, and got multiple offers, some of which offered 50 percent to 70 percent pay increases. Surprisingly, I didn't take any of them. I know this sounds stupid. In fact, I felt stupid at the time. My gut told me not to, and my heart just wasn't into leaving. The timing wasn't right. I couldn't quite divorce with my husband either. Frankly, I found it difficult to make decisions about anything.

Vanessa: What changed?

Angela: The turning point came when I realized I was heading for a breakdown. I knew I could no longer shoulder all of this myself, but I didn't know what to do. I was mad, angry, and sick all the time. I vacillated from divorcing my husband to staying. We decided to go to counseling. In counseling I realized that I was just burned out. I hadn't cultivated support systems at work or at home. I realized that I was trying to live up to an image of what I thought I should be—Superwoman—and ignoring what I really was: overworked, out of shape, smart, loving, blessed with three kids, tired, and confused. I finally cut myself some slack and gave up that image of Superwoman. What a relief! In counseling I learned how to get support. I found a mentor to support me at work and a housekeeper to help on the homefront. I literally got my life and marriage back.

Vanessa: Sounds as if it was all coming together. So why did you decide to quit?

Angela: It was all falling into place. The quality of my work relationship and my marriage had improved beyond belief. Within the first year of making those changes, I got a promotion and was assigned the best clients in our region. My husband was more supportive, and we began to enjoy each other again.

Things were steadily improving, then WHAM! My mother was diagnosed with a terminal brain tumor. It scared the heck out of me. I can't explain how I felt. I was so afraid of losing my mother. This made me take a serious look at the way I was living my own life. I was still running a hundred miles an hour and wondering

	how long I could keep it up. I knew I had to make some changes. I wanted to be there for my kids, like Mom was for me.
Vanessa:	What did you do?
Angela:	I made myself set boundaries. In the past, I had always played the role of the archangel. This time I wasn't afraid to ask for support. I set clear expectations with my family to share in the caring for our mother. I shared the crisis with a few people at work and asked them to support me, and they did. That was crucial because I was in a lot of pain and not really focused on my job.

Waiting for Mom to die was excruciating. As I sat in her hospital room, I thought of how young she was—only 51—with so many things still to experience. I started thinking about all my dreams, deferred and lost. I knew that it was time to make a change.

Vanessa:	Is this when you decided to resign?
Angela:	Well, I was in the middle of deciding. I hadn't really made the final decision. When I would think about leaving, I felt so guilty. I didn't want to hurt or disappoint anyone. I also kept telling myself that I had finally gotten it right, so I should stay and enjoy it. I had access to the inner circle; I felt protected and safe. I was a role model for black women. The organization was making a commitment to deal with the myriad of issues affecting black women. I had everything I thought I wanted, yet I couldn't change this desire to leave. I instinctively knew more was out there for me. I guess you could say that my mom's death forced me to come to terms with the fact that my life was "not on purpose." I wasn't doing what I had passion for.
Vanessa:	What did you learn from all of this that would be helpful to our readers?
Angela:	Well, I really made several Smart Moves. First, I

took a break after Mom's funeral. I got my husband to care for the kids, and I took a week by
myself in the Caribbean. I spent time focusing
on myself while contemplating the gifts my
mother had given me during her lifetime [*Feed
the Source*].

Second, I had to accept my own decision to
leave and its consequences [*Own Your Choice*]. It
sounds easier than it felt at the time. I was so
nervous at first. I decided to start my own business. This meant a significant dent in our family's income. My husband was also quite
nervous; now financially everything was his responsibility. I also had to get comfortable with
the fact that he would be taking care of me for a
while. That was a weird feeling.

Next, I got all types of support [*Get Support*] to
get me through. I had always relied on Mom to
help me through my most personal issues. I
knew I had to find someone to fill this void. I
spent a lot of time getting clear about what I really wanted [*Visualize Your Choice*] and how I
needed to make it happen.

Finally, I crafted a personal plan [*Have a Plan
and Do It*] of what I needed to accomplish if this
was going to work. I made myself write it
down so it became very real. Then I began to
solicit support from my organization so that I
could leave on good terms. I started to concentrate on creating a business plan for my new
venture. Before I made my announcement at
work, I had everything in order [*Make Time Your
Ally*].

Vanessa: How did you go about severing your work rela-
             tionship?

Angela: I planned this out too. I wanted to be prepared
             for as many reactions as possible. I knew they
             would feel shocked, hurt, rejected, and maybe
             taken for granted. I took your suggestion and

made a list of their potential emotional reactions [*Anticipate Emotional Reactions*] and wrote out how I would respond. My objective was to tell them why this was so important for me at this moment in my life [*Know How to Tell Your Story*]. I told them I was starting my own business—doing something that I would feel passionate about. I wanted to reassure them that they did nothing to create my decision to leave. I shared with them how I'd grown as a result of being a part of their family. I also shared how much the organization's commitment to address the issues of black women had meant to me personally and how I felt the organization had grown in the diversity issue.

Luckily, just at the time I was about to resign, the company announced its intent to cut back on personnel. For obvious reasons, I wanted to volunteer to leave and get a severance package. A year's salary would be an incredible boost for me. Again, I used the techniques that I had used earlier: I did my homework, I got clear about what I wanted, and I enrolled key people in the company to support me. I got all the separation benefits and agreed to stay one month longer to select and train my replacement. Everybody was happy.

Vanessa: Well, today's a celebration day for you then! Sounds to me that you've done a lot of hard work. If you could leave one important thought or lesson with our readers, what would it be?

Angela: The most important thing is to be honest with yourself and be very clear about what it is you want to do in life. Don't forget to feed the source. Once you do these two things, you can make anything happen.

Reconciling Differences and Falling in Love—Again: Gloria's Story

Gloria has just received her second promotion in nine months. She has broken the glass ceiling by moving from middle management into the senior management group. Now she is responsible for a five-state sales region, which contributes substantially to her company's volume and profit. Ironically, this same region was quite hostile to her earlier in her career. Now she feels that she's married to her company with all the benefits that come with her status. She's happy and fulfilled. This is great for her.

Vanessa:	Gloria, you seem like a newlywed. When you talk about Sales Co., you blush and smile. I noticed you use the word *we* all the time. You seem very genuine.
Gloria:	Absolutely. The feeling is genuine. I expect a lot more from the company as my career continues to progress. But I must tell you, I can't imagine another moment being as wonderful as this point in my life!
Vanessa:	Gloria, when you say "this point," it suggests to me that you've had less exhilarating experiences.
Gloria:	I'll say. I was ready to leave four years ago. I was so fed up and tired of trying to get the recognition I knew I'd earned. The sexism was rampant. I was one of the first five women ever hired to work in this region. This had been the last male bastion in the company. It was a tough nut to crack.
Vanessa:	Did you crack it?
Gloria:	I'd like to say I did—but I almost died trying. During that period, I lost an ovary, my husband, my hair, and some of my self-confidence. I don't like to wallow long on that experience. I

am the only woman out of the class of five that survived. The rest left long ago.

Vanessa: What made you tough it out?

Gloria: Me and Sales Co. have come a long way. We've gone through a lot together. What made me tough it out? Well, I really liked what I was doing. It was exciting and new, and I had never envisioned making that much money.

Vanessa: Are you saying you couldn't have done that same work somewhere else and made that kind of money with fewer problems? I just feel there's got to be more to it than the work and money.

Gloria: Yes, there is! It's ego! I saw myself, when I started, getting to a senior vice-president level. I believed that I could. I refused to let anyone force me out or tell me I couldn't get there. [She looks reflectively.] But it cost me a lot.

Vanessa: What specifically happened to make you stay? I understand ego was a big driver, but obviously something else had to happen.

Gloria: Yes, something did happen. Me. I decided that I wasn't being strategic enough. I was trying to fight all of these battles myself. There was no way I could have won. I had gotten caught up in my own self-importance and power.

I realized I had to work smarter. I needed a plan [*Have a Plan and Do It*] if I was going to stay. In my heart, I really wanted to stay with Sales Co., so I wrote a letter to the CEO of my company [*Know How to Tell Your Story*]. I shared my concern that the company was putting itself in a very vulnerable legal position regarding women in this region. I had calculated the costs to the company of the four women who had left—almost $500,000. I then requested a meeting to discuss what I felt needed to be done [*Negotiate for What You Want*]. Now, I can't believe my nerve. I knew this would create an uproar, so I called my immediate supervisor, told him what I did, and faxed him a copy of the memo. I told him to be truthful because I would be, no matter what. I felt I needed to take an uncompromising stand [*Own Your Choice*].

I got the meeting with my CEO and a host of others. I came to the meeting with a detailed plan on how to redress the issue. It had costs, timeline, benefits—everything [*Negotiate for What You Want*]. I articulated up front what they must be thinking about me at that very moment—politically naive, suicidal, not a team player [*Anticipate Emotional Reactions*]. I assured them I was none of these. I reaffirmed my loyalty to the company and shared my belief that leadership required risk taking, and it sometimes took an unconventional approach to get things done. The CEO listened and committed to take action.

I earned the respect of the person who mattered most—myself. I also gained the support of my CEO. He made several overtures for us to have lunch. I took advantage of that opportunity [*Make Time Your Ally*]. I wanted to get his support [*Get Support*] to put me on a fast career track and get me out of that region, which was full of resentment for me. I decided I was going to focus on my own agenda. I would start saving the world by saving myself [*Feed the Source*]. I shared my vision of what I could be and contribute to the company [*Know How to Tell Your Story*]. He agreed to sponsor me. He was instrumental in getting me transferred. He made it clear to others that I had the intellect and capacity and had already established a successful track record. Everyone knew that they were to provide the environment, support, supervision, and training for me to be successful. The rest is history. I worked hard to maintain his support and earn the support of his key managers.

That's when I started getting invitations to key managers' social functions. I got inspected by their wives, and I passed. They didn't perceive me as a threat. I fit in nicely. I got included in key meetings that folks at my level normally didn't get invited to. At each of their meetings, I made myself visible and I contributed. I also made it a point to meet people and let them get to know me.

Vanessa: This may seem very calculating to some women.

Gloria: No, it's being very strategic. I've been clear and committed to getting what I deserve. Do you know what's so nice?

Vanessa: No, what?

Gloria: I've finally hit my stride. I know what I'm doing, and it's not such a struggle anymore. I took my chances, made my stand, and found the support I needed to stay without sacrificing those things I've always believed. I feel I'm making a contribution, and I'm really happy.

8

Road Map to Success

You have to know what you want to get.

> Gertrude Stein, in *Meditations for Women*
> *Who Do Too Much*

To achieve, you need thought . . . you have to know what you are doing and that's real power.

> Ayn Rand, in *Meditations for Women Who Do Too Much*

You're the only one who truly knows what you want and where you're going, so you're the best equipped to draw the map to your destination. This is your journey, and it's going to continue to be a wonderful odyssey of self-renewal and growth. Just think about what you've already learned about yourself and the work relationship you are seeking. Now, it's simply a matter of putting your plan on paper and going for it.

Planning. Simple. Right? Ha! We asked ourselves if we knew anyone who really liked to plan. Our answer was that we know women who like to plan—everything but a plan for their own life! It's not always easy to summon the discipline to put all of your thoughts on paper and sketch out your future, so we've made this necessary step as easy as possible.

Think of this as preparation for an exciting expedition. You're going to a place you've never been before, so you want to make sure that you've thought of every contingency. You need to be well packed and ready for anything that comes your way. It's time to make a list of the things you'll be needing. To help you, we have included our own plans from career journeys we embarked on in the past. Have a look at them in preparation for filling out your own plan next.

Career Journey Plans

Jan's Plan: Stay and Be Happy

Jan was hired right out of college as the only female in a southern sales district for BestCo. Her first two years were highlighted by exceptional performance. She was awarded with two job promotions that put her ahead of her peers. She thought she would be with BestCo for her lifetime. It provided her the security and professional challenge she longed for. But over the next four years, she grew concerned that her career had slowed down. She went from an assignment that offered tremendous growth opportunities and visibility to a different assignment, which had been packaged and sold to her as a key career move. As she read the tea leaves, it was clear that this assignment wasn't advancing her career. She had been told that she was the next in line for a coveted district manager (DM) assignment, but repeatedly the "next" came and went to someone else. There was always an excuse why she didn't get the promotion.

Jan got fed up with the excuses and decided to force the issue of her promotion. She really wanted to stay with BestCo, but she felt she wasn't being treated fairly. She crafted a plan with the intention of staying but getting her needs met.

Jan's Plan to Stay and Be Happy

Vision/Dream/Choice/Picture. *I have a clear sense of what I want. To make this happen in my life, I will:*

- Be treated with respect in all my company relationships.
- Be recognized for my contributions by a promotion to DM, either with BestCo or with another company.

- Help shape a sales culture that shares my values and advances people based on merit.
- Have contentment and peace in my life.

How Will I Know It's Right for Me? *I know it is natural to second-guess my decision. To minimize the time that I spend doing this I will:*

- Feel good about my contributions.
- Be a fun person for others to be around.
- Experience less stress in my life.
- Have strong, supportive personal and work relationships.
- Be living by my principles and values.

Action Steps   *Timing*

Own My Choice. *My preference is to stay with BestCo; however, I'm prepared to leave immediately if I don't receive:*

- Support by senior management commen-
  surate with my performance.   by 9/1
- My promotion to DM within one month.   by 10/1
- A salary increase.   by 10/1
- I will state my decision emphatically.
  I have a backup offer if each of these
  conditions isn't met.

Feed the Source. *There are certain things that I need to do for myself during this difficult period. I will:*

- Hire a personal trainer to work out with me.   √done
- Exercise each day to help manage my stress.   √doing
- Schedule a vacation in Mexico for R&R.   9/15
- Continue to develop supportive friends
  inside and outside BestCo.   √doing

Getting Support. *I want help and support so I will:*

- Surround myself with friends who care
  about me and communicate caring messages
  (Ramona, Shawn, Ron).   √doing
- Enroll the support of my mentor (Joe) to
  help me work my strategy to get what I want.   √done
- Recognize the efforts of people at work
  who help me (Joe, Lou).   √doing

Emotional Reactions. *I know that I need to focus on the reactions that I will feel and the reactions of others. To be prepared for this I will:*

- Stand firm despite the reactions of others.
- Not allow myself to get drawn into a finger-pointing, blaming match.
- Anticipate that my immediate supervisor will be very nervous, then angry.
- Reaffirm my desire to stay but be clear about my conditions to stay.

Negotiate. *I am prepared to negotiate as follows:*

- These conditions are nonnegotiable:
  —support by senior management commensurate
  with my performance   by 9/1
  —my promotion to DM within one month   by 10/1
  —a salary increase   by 10/1
- These conditions are negotiable:
  —city of DM position
  —percentage salary increase
  —supervisor
- The written job offer I have from Company Y shows a salary offer almost double what I'm currently making. The position Company Y is offering is more advanced than the DM position I'm seeking.

My Story. *I will tell my story as follows:*

I have been very patient and trusting regarding the management of my career. I have repeatedly attempted to address my career needs, yet I continue to get the runaround. There is always an excuse for why I didn't get promoted even though my contributions have consistently been assessed as "exceptional" throughout my six-year career.

I will no longer accept this treatment. I have a job offer from Company Y that puts me above the DM level and almost doubles my salary. I want to stay with BestCo. I sincerely want this relationship to work. However, my conditions have to be met for me to stay.

Getting Centered. *I know I need to keep my head and my heart focused, so . . .*

- If my conditions are met, I will do my part to make it work. I will celebrate.
- If my conditions are not met, I won't lose energy by blaming my-

self or getting angry because BestCo made a choice I don't value.

- I will go to Company Y, knowing that I have made the best choice for me. I will make it work. I will celebrate.
- Whether I stay or leave, I will make sure others know of my expectations of their role in supporting my career.
- I will take care of my emotional and physical selves because I am important.

Vanessa's Plan: Leave and Be Happy

The company had indicated that Vanessa would have to relocate to corporate headquarters because her field assignment was completed. She chose not to relocate. Rather, the timing seemed right to leave her work relationship of twelve and a half years. She wanted her leaving to be a win-win situation for her and the organization and decided to tie her leaving with the company's push to reduce its staff. She crafted a plan.

Vanessa's Plan to Leave and Be Happy

Vision/Dream/Choice/Picture. *I have a clear sense of what I want. To make this happen in my life I will:*

- Have a successful consulting practice that focuses on diversity, organizational restructuring, downsizing, and business therapies.
- Be the captain of my own ship. It'll be fun. I'll feel invigorated.
- Have a small staff of employees who feel energized and a part of building a new business. My family will be employees in my practice.
- Have more time to put against my marriage. I will travel more with my husband.

How Do I Know This Is Right for Me? *I know it is natural to second-guess my decision. To minimize the time that I spend doing this I will:*

- Feel passionate about what I'm doing.
- Feel very energized: I will get up early and be at the office.
- Have clients who pay for my services.
- Have creative approaches to my clients' needs.
- Do more fun things with my husband.

- Spend more time with my parents, children, and grandchild.

Action Steps	*Timing*

Owning My Choice. *My preference is to* leave with a package. *I am prepared to:*

- Leave with or without a separation package by   4/1 next yr
- I am not willing to relocate.

Feed the Source. *There are certain things that I need to do for myself during this difficult period. I will:*

- Focus on getting me healthy.   Immediately
- Reestablish relationships with my old friends.   10/1
- Travel only five days a month.
- Buy a new wardrobe.   1/1
- Only take clients who are committed to
  do things the right way versus the expedient way. 1/1
- Take a vacation every three months.   6/1

Getting Support. *I want help and support so I will:*

- Ask inside resources how to get a
  separation package.   by 10/15
- Get immediate supervisor's support.   11/1
- Enroll my husband and family in my vision
  and ask for their ideas on how I should start
  my business.   11/1
- Ask associates for business referrals.   12/1
- Get my friends to exercise with me.   √doing

Emotional Reactions. *I know that I need to focus on the reactions that I will feel and the reactions of others. To be prepared for this, I will:*

- Show my management how this benefits their agenda.
- Have a plan for my internal customers so they can continue my project with ease.
- Schedule special meetings with blacks and women who will be concerned about losing their management advocate. I will address their issues then.

Negotiate. *I am prepared to negotiate as follows:*

- Demonstrate how my voluntary resignation helps achieve my

supervisor's staff reduction goal and minimizes someone else's pain.

- My voluntary resignation is contingent on my getting a separation package.
- Create an opportunity to have Company X as a client.

My Story. *I will tell my story as follows:*

My field assignment was cut short because of the company's new business direction. The absence of assignments in Los Angeles requires me to relocate to corporate headquarters in the Midwest. I am married, and it's not feasible for my husband to relocate his medical practice. I do not want a commuter marriage. The only practical option is for me to leave this work relationship. I'm happy with this option; however, I'll need to move out of this work relationship with a separation package.

Getting Centered. *I know I need to keep my head and my heart focused, so . . .*

- I accept that even with the best-laid plans, cutting the umbilical cord creates some anxiety. It's normal. I believe I will make it in these tough economic times.
- I affirm that I have taken the right steps to launch my business.
- I will give to others so I don't become self-absorbed in only my business.

Your Turn

Take some time, say an hour or so, and fill in the blank form that follows. Think about how one hour of planning can spare you hundreds of hours of grief. When you consider that you work an average of 2,000 hours or more a year, this one-hour investment can pay huge dividends! Refer back to the Smart Moves exercises you did in the last chapter to help you piece your plan together.

_____Plan To_____

Vision/Dream/Choice/Picture. *I have a clear sense of what I want. To make this happen in my life I will:*

-
-
-
-
-

How Do I Know This Is Right for Me? *I know it is natural to second-guess my decision. To minimize the time that I spend doing this I will:*

-
-
-
-
-

Action Steps   *Timing*

Owning My Choice. *My preference is to_____.*
I'm prepared to:

-
-
-
-
-

Feed the Source. *There are certain things that I need to do for myself during this difficult period. I will:*

-
-
-
-

Emotional Reactions. *I know that I need to focus on the reactions that I will feel and the reactions of others. To be prepared for this I will:*

-
-
-
-
-

Negotiate. *I am prepared to negotiate as follows:*

-
-
-
-
-

My Story. *I will tell my story (in 100 words or less) as follows:*

Getting Centered. *I know I need to keep my head and my heart focused, so:*

-
-
-
-
-

Dangerous Curves

Putting your plan on paper will not make it happen. You have to put your car on the road and drive. But before you take off, we want to warn you about a few of the dangerous curves you're likely to encounter on your road to work relationship success. Everybody will have a reaction to your plan and to your choices. Some people will be surprisingly supportive, and some will be devastatingly nasty. Although we thought we were prepared for the emotional reactions we would encounter, we were still caught off-guard by some of the challenging comments people made—either to our faces or behind our backs. When that happened, we were distracted from our plan and were tempted to react by justifying, defending, and, in some cases, retaliating with our own unkind words. We knew that wouldn't be a Smart Move, so we just bit our tongues. In retrospect, we thought of things we wished we'd said. We've captured those thoughts here so that you can consider them as you prepare for the emotional reactions you will encounter. The following two sections identify the emotional reactions to both staying and leaving.

Emotional Reactions to Staying

You may be surprised by your own unexpected emotions as you reenter your work relationship with a renewed energy to make it fulfilling. Some of the following reactions could apply to you:

- *Fear/second thoughts*—"Is this the right move?"
- *Paranoia*—"Can I really trust that they'll do what they say they will?"
- *Relief*—"I'm glad I've made this decision. Now we can get on with things."
- *Euphoria*—"I'm getting what I wanted all along!"
- *Caution*—"I'll be more careful now that I know what I know. I have to set better boundaries for this relationship so I don't run into trouble again."
- *Thrilled*—"I've just made it through what feels like a critical rite of passage in my work relationship. I'm a veteran now. I'm not so naive anymore, and people treat me with more respect now."
- *Confidence*—"I'm ready to start having fun now that people understand what I want and are willing to support me so I get it."

Others' reactions can throw you off course and leave you feeling defensive, angry, distracted, or, in some case, surprisingly happy. The key is for you to keep your calm no matter what happens. Practice these Smart Women responses in your own words:

Angry—"After all your complaints, why are you still putting up with that crap? I'd be outta there!"

Smart Woman response: "I'm staying because I don't see myself as a victim anymore. Instead, I realize that I have choices. I'm going to stop complaining because I have a plan to make this relationship work. I'm giving myself six months to turn it around, and if I can't work it out, I *will* leave. But I'd like your support in the meantime."

Surprised—"I never even knew you had an issue with us until you began talking about leaving."

Smart Woman response: "I'm glad that now you do understand how important these issues are to me. I really want this relationship to work, but I need to get my needs met as well. What I've learned is that I have to press harder to be heard, particularly when I feel that what I've communicated has been discounted or dismissed."

Relief—"Whew, I thought you were gonna leave."

Smart Woman response: "I was afraid I was going to have to leave too, but I'm glad we've worked this out. Sometime soon let's talk about what we've learned from all of this so our relationship never gets to this point again."

Suspicion—"You've talked about leaving. How can we know that you are truly committed to this work relationship?"

Smart Woman response: "The important thing is that you and I are clear about what it takes for us *both* to be committed to the success of this work relationship. I'll take the first step to share what I'm willing to do to make it work, but then I'd like to hear what you're willing to do. After all, we're both in this together."

Envy—"How did you negotiate that great job when so many other people are losing theirs?"

Smart Woman response: "Help me better understand the intent of your question. Do you want to know my strategy, or are you saying you're happy for me?"

Celebration—"You finally got what you wanted; let's celebrate!"

Smart Woman response: "It's great to know that I have people like you who understand and celebrate my choices. I've appreciated your support. This has been a tough time for me. Now, let's party."

Genuine support—"Let me know what I can do to help you. I don't want to lose you."

Smart Woman response: "I'm really glad to know you feel that way, and it's that kind of attitude that's contributed to my decision to stay. Now that I've been through all of this and know I have your support, I won't be so shy about asking for your help in the future."

Respect—"I appreciate that you're taking responsibility to make this relationship work. So many other people just complain or leave without giving us a chance to make things right. I've learned a lot about you through this process."

Smart Woman response: "Thanks. I've learned a lot of good and special things about you too. Wouldn't it be fun if we could get together for lunch on a regular basis? Why don't I set it up for Friday?"

Anytime you've considered leaving a relationship, you've exposed a vulnerability in the relationship that can wear like a worn tire, and either you or your partner feels vulnerable. If you were the one who threatened to leave the relationship, your partner may have a hard time accepting that you are really committed to staying and will be more cautious about your relationship. You'll have to work hard to regain trust by behaving in a way that supports your commitment to the relationship. If you doubted whether you should stay because your partner compromised you in some way, then you will always have a vulnerability to that issue. If the issues that caused the friction continually reappear, you will have a blow-out, and your relationship may suffer irreparable damage.

Emotional Reactions to Leaving

In many ways, leaving can be more emotionally draining than staying. Typically you are leaving behind people and relationships that have been part of the fabric of your life. You will experience a range of emotions, so prepare yourself by understanding reactions you already feel, as well as those that you've experienced when you ended a close personal relationship in the past:

- *Fear/second thoughts*—"Is this the right move?"
- *Paranoia*—"They're saying bad things about me as I walk out the door."
- *Relief*—"Thank goodness it's finally over!"
- *Euphoria*—"I'm free at last!"
- *Revenge*—"Take this job and shove it!"
- *Pride*—"I did it my way."
- *Shock*—"Wow, it's really over. There's no going back."
- *Pain*—"I guess I wasn't as important to them as I thought I was."
- *Poetic justice*—"They got what they deserved."
- *Caution*—"I'll never care that much again for any job."
- *Sadness*—"I'm leaving behind people and projects I cared about."
- *Loss*—"I thought those people were my friends. Now I see that they were just coworkers."
- *Betrayal*—"They didn't live up to their promises. They left me no other choice but to leave."
- *Loneliness*—"It's all up to me now. I'm all alone."
- *Confidence*—"I can do whatever I want. I'm no longer tied down by a work relationship that doesn't work for me. I create my future!"

Your choice can be an emotionally charged issue for others as well:

Envy—"You're doing what I wish I had the guts to do!"

Smart Woman response: "Thanks for the compliment."

Anger—"How could you do this to us after all we've done for you?!"

Smart Woman response: "I can understand why you feel angry about my decision to leave, but there comes a time in life when you have to put your own needs ahead of everyone else's and follow your instincts. I've got to do that now. I'm sorry things haven't worked out as we had once planned. You may not be able to hear this now, but I sincerely appreciate all that you have personally done for me. This hasn't been an easy choice for me, and I hope that one day you can understand why I've had to make it for myself."

Inadequacy—"Why couldn't I convince you to stay and work things out?"

Smart Woman response: "You know, this was a tough decision, and I made it based on what was right for me. I have too much respect for our friendship to put you in a position of trying to convince me to do something that just isn't right for me. I appreciate that you care, and I know that you've done all that you can to help me. Help me now by respecting my choice."

Rejection—"You made your choice. You left us, we didn't leave you, so there's nothing left for us to talk about."

Smart Woman response: "I'm sorry you feel that way, but at least I know where you stand. If you ever change your mind and feel like talking about it, I'm here."

Abandoned—"I thought you were the one who was going to change things for the better around here. Why are you leaving us when we need you?"

Smart Woman response: "It means a lot to me that you recognize that I worked hard to improve things. But I feel even better knowing that you have the ability to continue on with the work we started."

Genuine support—"You're doing what's best for you. You'll find your way, and it will be better than ever before."

Smart Woman response: "You are really a special friend. So many other people have been trying to tell me what *they* think is right for me, but not you. You've encouraged me to make my own decisions, and your confidence in my judgment has helped me through this tough time."

Genuine concern—"You and I go back a long way, and I have to tell you that I think you're making a mistake. You know that I have your best interests at heart."

Smart Woman response: "I know that you care about me, and I have to admit that I've thought a lot about whether this truly is the right choice for me. I haven't made this decision lightly. But now that I've made it, I own it, and I'm going to do everything I can to make it work. I hope that although I'm leaving, we can continue with our friendship."

Bargaining—"I know you're leaving, but can you please stay until . . . "

Smart Woman response: "Yes, I'm willing to stay for (x) time under these conditions, but after that I must leave." Or, "I appreciate your asking me to stay, but it's really time for me to go. I just can't stay any longer than two weeks. But what I can do before I go is help you map out a plan to continue my work/project. I'd really like to do that."

Finally, there are two reactions for which we have no Smart Woman response:

- *Relief*—"Whew, I thought she'd never leave!"
- *Nastiness*—"I never liked her anyway! I don't know how she ever got to where she was. She wasn't that good."

The reason there is no response is that typically these reactions are never expressed directly to you. They are part of the conversations designed to complete the burying of your memory and presence in the organization. We call this the "organizational funeral."

The organizational funeral is a set of rituals the organization goes through to "get okay" with an ended relationship. Every organization has its funeral ritual. When the work relationship ends amicably, the organizational funeral consists of going-away lunches and dinners, with gifts, hugs, and best wishes. This funeral is really a celebration of your ascent to your next life.

When the relationship ends tersely, it's an entirely different matter. Your name is immediately removed from your office door, files are locked, people treat you suspiciously. You are stripped of all company identification. You have to sign exit documents. People talk negatively about you, and rarely do others stick their neck out to defend your honor. You stop getting invitations to colleagues' homes. It's almost as if you have a disease that your past associates are afraid to catch, so they don't come around. You simply get buried and cease to exist.

Be prepared for this funeral ritual, because it's possibly the most shocking of your leaving experiences. You need to realize and accept that this may happen, and there's not much you can or should do about it. Stay focused on why you left and surround yourself with people who understand your vision and offer genuine support. We offer an affirmation for you to carry with you for this experience: "I keep the telephone of my mind open to peace, harmony, health, love and abundance. Then whenever doubt, anxiety, or fear try to call me, they keep getting a busy signal and soon they'll forget my number."[1]

9

Endings and New Beginnings

> By allowing yourself to know that every [work] relation-
> ship not only invites you but propels you into the future,
> you can face what felt like the frighteningly uncharted ter-
> ritory of your future with a new-found sense of direction,
> confidence, optimism and excitement.
>
> Daphne Rose Kingma, *Coming Apart: Why Relationships
> End and How to Live Through the Ending of Yours*

It's time to celebrate. You've come a long way on your journey
to forge a work relationship that's right for you. Remember
your thoughts when you first picked up this book? Just think
about how much you've learned about yourself and your
choices. There's been a lot in this book about relationships, but
the important point to recognize is that the most profound relationship you have is the one with yourself. When you are clear
about what motivates you—what you value and believe—you
are free to make the choices that are within your control. Your
decisions and choices are motivated internally by you, not ex-
ternally by someone or something else. With that in mind, realize that the answers have always been within you. *Smart
Women, Smart Moves* merely provided a path for you to discover
and clarify what you wanted in your work relationship. You
empowered yourself to make it happen. Now it's time to pause

and celebrate the courageous steps you have taken to live life on your own terms.

In our busy lives, we don't often indulge in self-celebration. We're so quickly on to the next hurdle that we miss an important step of celebrating by capturing and cataloging the lessons we've learned. This is a crucial step in the process:

- You deserve a moment to stop and celebrate how wonderful you are.
- Only by realizing what you've learned will you be able to apply what you know to future circumstances.
- Knowledge is power. Knowing that you can navigate your way through a troubled work relationship will give you strength and power to get through the tough spots when your relationship troubles you in the future.

Wrap Party

At the end of big productions and events, it is customary to "wrap" the event by having a party to celebrate and to reflect on everything that happened along the way. Let's hold a wrap party. Like snapshots, you'll remember times you were laughing at yourself, and sometimes you'll recall poignant moments when you overcame past challenges. In recalling your journey, celebrate the steps you took in each chapter toward creating the work relationship you want and deserve.

Since you started your journey, you've acquired a treasure chest of tools that can be continuously reapplied to evaluate the work relationships you'll establish over a lifetime. Let's recap.

The Feminine Relationship Model may be used as a basis to discuss the kind of relationship you have and to clarify with your employer or clients what it will take to have the relationship you both want. We found that men can relate to this model and welcome an opportunity to discuss their needs, wishes, and boundaries for a work relationship with you. In fact, they're relieved to have this open discussion. You might even have your immediate supervisor, who is one of your most intimate work relationships, take the Work Relationship Indicator—Parts I and II as if they

were you, and also for themselves. This exercise will spark discussion and can be the first step in creating a more meaningful
work relationship.

You will hit snags in your relationship, but you now know
that trouble in paradise doesn't mean trouble forever. You've
faced the fear that your relationship may be in trouble and needs
to end or change drastically. Use the trouble in paradise list of
warning signs in Chapter 3 to sort out what you may be feeling.
We suggest that you look at these warning signs whenever you
feel that something isn't right with your work relationship. Review these emotional reactions to help you determine how se-
vere your trouble may be so you can do something about it.

The Message Quiz can be used in the future to see if and
where there is imbalance in your life and what that will mean if
you don't create other choices for balance. Take this quiz whenever you start feeling signs of stress in your life. It will help you
pinpoint the source of stress so that you can take appropriate
steps to alleviate it.

Go back often and repeat the visualization exercises in
Chapter 5 as a means of staying in touch with your inner values
and dreams. We strongly encourage this because we've seen its
power when it's earnestly done. The value of this exercise is to
focus on the possibilities of what your work relationship, in the
context of your life, can be.

We've spent time looking at choices. You realized that it is
by thinking, but principally by doing, that you create the work
relationships that you want. You also verified the importance of
your intuition and feelings. You know that your body gives you
strong signals and often tells you what your mind so many
times refuses to acknowledge. We strongly suggest you use the
Choice Quiz before leaving or starting a new work relationship.

And finally, continually apply the ten Smart Moves in your
life. Remember that everyone won't celebrate your choices. The
resistance you feel from them is their issue; don't make it yours.
When you encounter their resistance, simply refer to your
Smart Women responses and move on. Keep focused on your
plan, and surround yourself with people who support your en-
deavors.

Final Thoughts

Jot down some of the thoughts and feelings that you are experiencing at this moment. Since relationships aren't always smooth sailing, it might be helpful for you in the future if you were able to look back and reread the words you'll write now. In this way, you'll be able to call to mind the excitement and energy you feel as you embark on a new beginning.

I am celebrating because I have _____

_____

_____

_____

_____

_____.

I've learned some things that I don't want to forget when the going gets good. These things are: _____

_____

_____

_____

_____.

If there are other thoughts you want to capture, write them below:

_____

_____

_____

_____

_____.

Our Thanks to You

Thanks for allowing us to share our experiences and ideas with you. We feel honored that you've allowed us to be a part of your world and life experiences. In the beginning of this book, we shared Merle Shain's words on friendship. We hope that we have in some way been able to "supply you with energy and hope" in our efforts to support the contributions of all working women.

Writing this book has also been a learning process for us. We began with a blazing desire to educate women on how to leave their work relationships with their self-confidence intact. But as we examined our own experiences and talked with countless numbers of women, we realized how much more this book is really about choice: a woman's right to choose and influence the quality of her work relationships.

We also recognized how important it is for each of us to care enough to share our experiences with others. In the process, we reaffirmed lessons we already knew and learned completely new ones. These are the personal lessons we experienced while writing *Smart Women, Smart Moves*:

- It's our right as women to demand as much from our work relationships as we put into those relationships.
- We must continuously be smart about what we want and smart about how we go after it.
- We're fortunate to live in a time when women have so much to choose from. Certainly the wealth of opportunities creates difficulties, but it's exciting to be able to make choices that are right for us.
- Once you've learned the skills to securing successful work relationships, no one can take those skills away from you.

As we close this final chapter, we leave you with one last simple tale that symbolizes the power of what we can accomplish when we keep a clear vision, persevere, and never settle for less than we deserve:

The coast was shrouded in fog that fourth of July morning in 1952. Twenty-one miles to the west on Catalina Island, a 34-year-old woman waded into the water and began swimming toward the mainland, determined to be the first woman to do so. Her name was Florence Chadwick, and she had already been the first woman to swim the English Channel in both directions.

The water was numbing cold that July morning, and the fog was so thick she could hardly see the boats in her own party. Several times sharks had to be driven away with rifles. As the hours ticked off, she swam on. Fatigue had never been her big problem—it was the bone-chilling cold of the water.

Fifteen and one-half hours later, numbed with the cold, she asked to be taken out. She couldn't go on. Her mother and her trainer alongside in a boat told her they were near land. They urged her not to quit. But when she looked toward Long Beach, on the mainland, all she could see was the dense fog. After another twenty-five minutes—when she had been in the water almost sixteen hours—she quit and was lifted into the boat.

It was not until hours later, when her body began to thaw, that she felt the shock of failure. To a reporter she explained, "Look, I'm not excusing myself. But if I could have *seen* land, I might have made it."

After swimming over twenty miles of the twenty-one-mile channel, she had been pulled out only a half-mile from her goal! Later she was to reflect that she had been licked not by fatigue or even by the cold—but by the foggy coastline and the fuzzy images in her mind. She had no clear picture of her goal—nor of the path leading to that goal. The external and internal fog had blinded her reason, her eyes, and her heart.

It was the only time Florence Chadwick ever quit. Two months later she swam the same channel, and again the fog obscured her view, but this time she swam with a clear vision of her goal in her head—a mental map of where she was going. Not only was she the first woman to swim the Catalina Channel, but she beat the men's record by some two hours.[1]

Just like Florence Chadwick, we're sure you noticed that your confidence grew with each insight you gained and challenge you met. You found that you had strengths, skills, self-determination, and perseverance, the depths of which you just now realize. Now you see that painful experiences can also be periods of tremendous growth. Continue to celebrate yourself and your accomplishments.

Best of luck to you. Be choiceful, and continue being a Smart Woman who makes very Smart Moves.

Notes

Introduction

1. Merle Shain, *When Lovers Are Friends* (New York: Bantam Books, 1978).
2. Jane Ciabarrari, "Managing Nine Critical Career Turning Points," *Working Woman* (October 1987), p. 37.
3. Ibid.
4. Ibid.

Part I. Work Relationship: The Female Perspective

1. Patricia Aburdene and John Naisbitt, *Megatrends for Women* (New York: Villard Books, 1992).

Chapter 1. It's More Than a Job; It's a Relationship

1. Stanley W. Cloud, "Standing Tall: The Capital Is All Agog at the New Attorney General's Outspoken Honesty," *Time*, May 10, 1993, p. 46.

Chapter 4. Problems Are Messages

1. William Glasser, *Control Theory: A New Explanation of How We Control Our Lives* (New York: Harper & Row, 1984).
2. *Workforce 2000* (Indianapolis: Hudson Institute, 1987).

Part III. Choice: At the Crossroads

1. Merle Shain, *When Lovers Are Friends* (New York: Bantam Books, 1978).

Chapter 5. What Do You Really Want?

1. Shakti Gawain, *Creative Visualization* (New York: Bantam Books, 1982), pp. 2–3.

Chapter 6. Celebrate or Take Off the Hat

1. William Glasser, *Control Theory: A New Explanation of How We Control Our LIves* (New York: Harper & Row, 1984).

Chapter 7. Smart Moves

1. Patricia Aburdene and John Naisbitt, *Megatrends for Women* (New York: Villard Books, 1992), pp. *xx*, 137.

2. From Procter & Gamble Distributing Company.

3. Iyania Vanzant, *Tapping the Power Within* (New York: Harlem River Press, 1992).

Chapter 8. Road Map to Success

1. Quoted in *Great Quotes From Great Women* (Lombard, Ill.: Great Quotations, Inc., no date cited).

Chapter 9. Endings and New Beginnings

1. Norma Carr-Ruffino, *The Promotable Woman* (Belmont, Calif.: Wadsworth Publishing, 1993), adapted from *Bits & Pieces*, ed. by Marvin G. Gregory (Fairfield, N.J.: The Economics Press, 1979).

Index